IF FO

MW01282320

👤 _____

✉ _____
   _____

📱 _____

Greater Than a Tourist Book Series
Reviews from Readers

I think the series is wonderful and beneficial for tourists to get information before visiting the city.

-Seckin Zumbul, Izmir Turkey

I am a world traveler who has read many trip guides but this one really made a difference for me. I would call it a heartfelt creation of a local guide expert instead of just a guide.

-Susy, Isla Holbox, Mexico

New to the area like me, this is a must have!

-Joe, Bloomington, USA

This is a good series that gets down to it when looking for things to do at your destination without having to read a novel for just a few ideas.

-Rachel, Monterey, USA

Good information to have to plan my trip to this destination.

-Pennie Farrell, Mexico

Great ideas for a port day.

-Mary Martin USA

Aptly titled, you won't just be a tourist after reading this book. You'll be greater than a tourist!

-Alan Warner, Grand Rapids, USA

Even though I only have three days to spend in San Miguel in an upcoming visit, I will use the author's suggestions to guide some of my time there. An easy read - with chapters named to guide me in directions I want to go.

-Robert Catapano, USA

Great insights from a local perspective!

Useful information and a very good value!

-Sarah, USA

This series provides an in-depth experience through the eyes of a local. Reading these series will help you to travel the city in with confidence and it'll make your journey a unique one.

-Andrew Teoh, Ipoh, Malaysia

GREATER THAN A TOURIST-NEW MEXICO USA

50 Travel Tips from a Local

Jeff Christensen

CZYK Publishing Since 2011.

Greater Than a Tourist
Visit our website at www.GreaterThanaTourist.com

Lock Haven, PA
All rights reserved.
ISBN: 9781794616783

>TOURIST

50 TRAVEL TIPS FROM A LOCAL

BOOK DESCRIPTION

Are you excited about planning your next trip?

Do you want to try something new?

Would you like some guidance from a local?

If you answered yes to any of these questions, then this Greater Than a Tourist book is for you.

Greater Than a Tourist- New Mexico, USA, by Jeff Christensen offers the inside scoop on America's 47th state. Most travel books tell you how to travel like a tourist. Although there is nothing wrong with that, as part of the Greater Than a Tourist series, this book will give you travel tips from someone who has lived at your next travel destination.

In these pages, you will discover advice that will help you throughout your stay. This book will not tell you exact addresses or store hours but instead will give you excitement and knowledge from a local that you may not find in other smaller print travel books.

Travel like a local. Slow down, stay in one place, and get to know the people and the culture. By the time you finish this book, you will be eager and prepared to travel to your next destination.

TABLE OF CONTENTS

BOOK DESCRIPTION
TABLE OF CONTENTS
DEDICATION
ABOUT THE AUTHOR
HOW TO USE THIS BOOK
FROM THE PUBLISHER
OUR STORY
WELCOME TO
> TOURIST
1. INTRODUCING NEW MEXICO
2. NO, AMERICANS DON'T NEED A PASSPORT
   TO COME HERE
3. SPLIT DOWN THE MIDDLE: A LESSON IN
   NEW MEXICO GEOGRAPHY
4. THE BEST TIMES TO TRAVEL: AN
   INTRODUCTION TO NEW MEXICO'S
   FAIRLY CONSISTENT CLIMATE
5. GETTING THERE AND AROUND
6. THERE'S AN APP FOR THAT
7. XERISCAPING: NEW MEXICO'S APPROACH
   TO LANDSCAPING
8. TAKE A DEEP BREATH AND LATHER UP
9. DON'T GET CARRIED AWAY
10. YOU MAY FIND THIS SHOCKING, BUT…

11. AVOID BECOMING AN ACCIDENTAL TOURIST

12. CLOSE ENCOUNTERS OF THE DEADLY KIND

13. PUT OUT OR GET OUT

14. SMOKEY BEAR: A STAR IS BORN

15. A NEW MEXICO STATE OF MIND

16. THE LIFE-SAVING YUCCA PLANT

17. YES, ROADRUNNERS ARE REAL!

18. OUR AWARD-WINNING FLAG

19. OUR PEOPLE: EVERYBODY IS SOMEBODY IN NEW MEXICO

20. OUR LANGUAGES: A UNIQUE BLEND OF CULTURES AND VOCABULARIES

21. OUR CODE WORDS: HOW TO SPEAK LIKE A NATIVE

22. OUR CLOTHING: WARDROBE ESSENTIALS FOR FASHIONISTAS

23. DON'T FAKE IT: HOW TO MAKE SURE TURQUOISE JEWELRY IS REAL

24. OUR INDIAN TRIBES

25. WHY DO INDIAN RESERVATIONS LOOK LIKE THIRD WORLD COUNTRIES?

26. THE CURSE OF COMMUNAL LAND

27. FREEDOM, OPPORTUNITY OR BONDAGE WITH EASE? YOU PICK.

28. TOP 5 PLACES TO EXPERIENCE NATIVE AMERICAN CULTURE

29. TOP 5 PLACES TO BUY NATIVE AMERICAN SOUVENIRS

30. TOP 5 PLACES TO SEE PETROGLYPHS

31. OUR FOOD: IT'S CALLED 'NEW MEX', NOT 'TEX MEX'

32. CHILE OR CHILI?

33. RED OR GREEN?

34. TOP 5 NEW MEXICAN FOODS YOU HAVE TO TRY

35. TOP 5 NATIVE AMERICAN FOODS YOU HAVE TO TRY

36. TOP 5 NEW MEXICAN SWEET-TOOTH SATISFIERS

37. TOP 5 RESTAURANTS THAT OFFER A TRULY NEW MEXICAN EXPERIENCE

38. TOP 5 DRINKS TO WASH IT ALL DOWN

39. TOP 5 PLACES TO STAY FOR A TRULY NEW MEXICAN EXPERIENCE

40. THE NEW MEXICO ART SCENE: TOP 3 PLACES TO EXPERIENCE NEW MEXICAN ART

41. PARTY LIKE A NEW MEXICAN: THE STATE'S TOP 5 FESTIVALS

42. TOP 5 SITES THAT ARE SHROUDED IN MYSTERY

43. TOP 5 OTHERWORLDLY LANDSCAPES

44. TOP 5 'OTHER' OUTDOOR PLACES TO EXPLORE

45. TOP 5 KITSCHY CURIOSITIES WORTH A PHOTO (OR A LISTEN)

46. TOP 5 PLACES TO EXPERIENCE THE WILD WEST

47. TOP 5 MUST-SEE HISTORICAL MARKERS

48. FOUR CORNERS IS OFF-MARK (BUT SO WHAT?)

49. TAKE YOUR PIC: NEW MEXICO'S 5 MOST PHOTOGENIC TOWNS

50. AMERICA'S SUNSET CAPITAL: TOP 5 PLACES TO WATCH THE SUN GO DOWN

TOP REASONS TO BOOK THIS TRIP

50 THINGS TO KNOW ABOUT PACKING LIGHT FOR TRAVEL

Packing and Planning Tips

Travel Questions

Travel Bucket List

NOTES

DEDICATION

This book is dedicated to my paternal great-grandfather and my maternal great-great grandparents who bravely left their native lands to settle the harsh New Mexico Territory. I am likewise grateful to my parents for raising me in such a unique and privileged place. Most importantly, I would like to thank my beautiful wife, Debbie, and my three adorable children, Chloe, Jonah & Maren, for encouraging me to live my dreams and for letting me cart them all over the world on my wild and crazy adventures.

ABOUT THE AUTHOR

Jeff Christensen is an author, songwriter, language and culture advisor, international presenter, online tourism instructor, and intrepid world traveler. Born and raised in Farmington, New Mexico, Jeff developed an incurable case of wanderlust at an early age. His travels have taken him to nearly 90 countries on six continents, but his heart still belongs to his beloved home state.

Jeff is a firm believer that travel opens eyes, hearts, and minds. He looks forward to introducing you to his all-time favorite state—New Mexico!

HOW TO USE THIS BOOK

The Greater Than a Tourist book series was written by someone who has lived in an area for over three months. The goal of this book is to help travelers either dream or experience different locations by providing opinions from a local. The author has made suggestions based on their own experiences. Please do your own research before traveling to the area in case the suggested places are unavailable.

Travel Advisories: As a first step in planning any trip abroad, check the Travel Advisories for your intended destination.
https://travel.state.gov/content/travel/en/traveladvisories/traveladvisories.html

FROM THE PUBLISHER

Traveling can be one of the most important parts of a person's life. The anticipation and memories that you have are some of the best. As a publisher of the Greater Than a Tourist book series, as well as the popular 50 Things to Know book series, we strive to help you learn about new places, spark your imagination, and inspire you. Wherever you are and whatever you do I wish you safe, fun, and inspiring travel.

Lisa Rusczyk Ed. D.
CZYK Publishing

OUR STORY

Traveling is a passion of the "Greater than a Tourist" series creator. Lisa studied abroad in college, and for their honeymoon Lisa and her husband toured Europe. During her travels to Malta, an older man tried to give her some advice based on his own experience living on the island since he was a young boy. She was not sure if she should talk to the stranger but was interested in his advice. When traveling to some places she was wary to talk to locals because she was afraid that they weren't being genuine. Through her travels, Lisa learned how much locals had to share with tourists. Lisa created the "Greater Than a Tourist" book series to help connect people with locals. A topic that locals are very passionate about sharing.

WELCOME TO
> TOURIST

1. INTRODUCING NEW MEXICO

*Twenty years from now you will
be more disappointed by the things
that you didn't do than by the ones
you did do. So throw off the
bowlines. Sail away from the safe
harbor. Catch the trade winds in
your sails. Explore. Dream.
Discover.*

– Mark Twain

*A ship in harbor is safe, but
that's not what ships are built for.*

– John A. Shedd

Once on a father-son road trip, my dad pointed out
two of northwestern New Mexico's most
recognizable landmarks—Ship Rock and Hogback.

Ship Rock was visible from my hometown of
Farmington 30 miles away, and Hogback—a lesser-
known sandstone hill that looks like a sow lying on
its belly—straddled the highway near the home where
my paternal grandmother was raised. My eleven-year-
old self had seen both of them often. This time,

13

however, was different, since my dad said something that struck me as odd.

"Did you know that people come from all over the world to see rock formations like these?" he asked. Studying the geologic features with a new sense of intrigue, I disbelievingly responded, "Why?"

My father owned a local moving and storage business that, among other things, shipped pieces of Native American art all over the country. I should have believed him, but growing up I failed to appreciate the incredible culture and beauty offered by the place I called home. It was only after leaving for a time that my eyes began to open. Attending graduate school in another country helped me realize how much I missed the sun, the sandstone, the juniper trees, the wide-open spaces, the air, the art, the accents, the festivals, the traditions, the people, and the food (oh, how I missed the food).

New Mexico is often referred to as a country within a country, and with good reason. It's a big state that packs a mighty big punch. Geographically, jaw-dropping landscapes abound at every turn, while culturally, the state's Native American, modern American, Spanish and Mexican heritages harmoniously meld together to create a beguiling blend of sights and smells you simply won't find anywhere else.

And so, it is with great pleasure that I introduce you to my amazingly rich and varied home state—a place I've always loved, but didn't always know it. Welcome to New Mexico!

2. NO, AMERICANS DON'T NEED A PASSPORT TO COME HERE

Even though New Mexico may seem like its own country, it really is a US state (#47, to be exact). This unique desert paradise joined the Union a full six weeks before Arizona and 47 years before Alaska & Hawaii. Yet sadly, poor New Mexico continues to suffer from Americans' geographic ignorance.

I remember when a friend tried to buy tickets to the 2002 Winter Olympics in Salt Lake City over the phone. As soon as he gave his New Mexico address to the operator, she promptly informed him that tickets were only available to US citizens. He insisted he *was* a US citizen and that New Mexico *was* indeed part of the country. She replied, "I understand you're from a US territory, sir, but these tickets are for citizens." What?!?!

Apparently, this particular friend was one of the lucky ones. At least the salesperson he spoke with knew that New Mexico was somehow affiliated with the United States, even if she mistakenly believed it was only a territory. Other New Mexican friends of mine were not so fortunate. When they tried to purchase Olympic tickets by phone, they were referred to the Mexican Consulate.

Over-the-phone ticketing agents aren't the only culprits. Bank tellers, cell phone providers, postal clerks, and every-day people on the street have all made similar gaffs. Once as children, my sisters and I were riding an out-of-state hotel elevator from our guestroom to the lobby. A friendly couple standing next to us asked where we were from. When we proudly responded, "New Mexico," they seemed puzzled then complimented us on our excellent English. We could only chuckle.

Another acquaintance once tried to mail a package home to New Mexico from another state and was charged foreign postage. Back in the early days of cell phones, some peoples' coverage was dropped the minute they crossed the New Mexico state line, only to be told by their carrier, "I'm sorry, but we don't offer service in Mexico." Then of course there's the story of a friend in Pennsylvania who received a wire transfer from her New Mexican parents for her birthday. A notice from her bank asked if she would like the money deposited in dollars or pesos.

Unbelievably, these types of situations happen to New Mexicans more often than you might think. The stories are so numerous that New Mexico Magazine, one of the state's longest running publications, used to print a monthly compilation of them.

If you take away only one thing from this book, please know that we're a state. Yes, a US state…and a pretty awesome one at that. You won't need a passport to come here. You won't need to change your money. You won't need to worry about roaming charges from your cell phone provider. Chances are you'll feel so at home in New Mexico, you may never want to leave.

3. SPLIT DOWN THE MIDDLE: A LESSON IN NEW MEXICO GEOGRAPHY

New Mexico is bisected by the 1,896-mile Rio Grande River that flows from Colorado to the Gulf of Mexico.

The state's northwest quadrant is Indian Territory—home to the Navajo Nation, the Jicarilla

Apache tribe, and a number of Pueblo communities. It's also where you'll find Four Corners National Monument—the only place in the United States where four states touch. Or is it? Read on.

In the northeast corner, pine-tree covered mountains give way to juniper-covered hills which in turn give way to dusty grasslands, punctuated every so often by ancient volcanic cones.

Southwest of the river lie bubbling hot springs, quirky towns, and Hatch—New Mexico's agricultural treasure.

To the river's southeast lies a desert so dry, it was dubbed by early Spanish explorers as 'Jornada del Muerto'. In English, that's roughly the equivalent of 'day-long journey of the dead.' No wonder scientists decided to detonate the world's first atomic bomb here.

But don't let that scare you. New Mexico's southeast quadrant is also home to the state's most iconic landmarks—the spellbinding White Sands National Monument (which isn't really sand but rather pulverized gypsum); the millennia-old Carlsbad Caverns National Park (which includes the country's deepest known limestone cave); and Roswell (a small desert town made famous by the rumored alien landings of 1947).

4. THE BEST TIMES TO TRAVEL: AN INTRODUCTION TO NEW MEXICO'S FAIRLY CONSISTENT CLIMATE

New Mexico—yes, the entire state—enjoys an average of 300 sunny days per year, making anytime a good time to visit.

Summers do bring monsoonal rains but even then, the state is relatively dry. Ruidoso, New Mexico's wettest city, averages 86 days of measurable precipitation each year with cumulative annual rainfall totaling less than 22 inches. Farmington, considered the driest major town in the state, receives less than 9 inches of precipitation across 62 days annually. Nearly one half of the state's annual rainfall occurs in July and August.

While the state is best known for its desert landscapes, it is also a popular ski destination. New Mexico is home to the southern-most peaks of the Rocky Mountains, and the Sangre de Cristo Range (part of the Rocky Mountain chain) offers excellent skiing at a fraction of the cost of resorts in neighboring Colorado. With phenomenal skiing in the north and warm, dry weather in the south, it's easy to understand why New Mexico is such a popular winter destination.

Summer temperatures across the state are comfortable and tend to fluctuate between 78°F (26°C) at higher elevations and 92°F (33°C) at lower elevations. The mercury rarely rises above 100°F (38°C) anywhere in New Mexico, and it's a dry, low-humidity heat when it does. Albuquerque, for example, has never experienced more than five days of >100°F (>38°C) temperatures in any given summer since 1995. Contrast that with the city of Phoenix in neighboring Arizona that has experienced an average of 110 days of >100°F (>38°C) heat each year since 1981.

In winter, expect average temperatures to be between 35°F (2°C) in the northern half of the state to 55°F (13°C) in the central and southern regions.

5. GETTING THERE AND AROUND

Getting In and Out

New Mexico's largest city, Albuquerque, isn't a hub for any major airline, which means the number of nonstop flights in and out of the state are limited. That doesn't mean there aren't any, though your flight choices may be fewer and farther between. Alaska, American, Delta, Frontier, JetBlue, Southwest, and United all offer nonstop flights to Albuquerque from a number of US cities. The Mexican airline, Volaris, also flies nonstop to Albuquerque from Guadalajara.

If you're planning to visit by car, three major interstate highways will help you get there:

- I-40, which runs east and west from North Carolina to California;

- I-25, which runs north and south from Wyoming to New Mexico;

- I-10, which runs east and west from California to Florida.

A number of well-maintained and not-so-well-maintained highways also crisscross the state, making all major points of interest fairly accessible.

One thing to note. While New Mexico conjures up images of seething desert landscapes, the central part of the state is actually quite mountainous and receives a decent amount of snow. Remember, the southern end of the Rocky Mountains spills over into the state and there are world-class ski resorts scattered throughout. Though rare, I-40 and I-25 can both experience blizzard conditions in the winter.

Getting Around Our Cities

If you don't plan to bring or rent your own car, you should know that public transportation and even taxi cabs are somewhat limited in our cities, though Uber and Lyft are allowed to operate unrestricted. Regardless, it's still best to have your own transportation in my mind. Please note, however, that parking can sometimes pose a challenge, especially in trendy tourist towns like Santa Fe.

Getting Around Our Countryside

New Mexico is the 5th largest state in the US, but one of the least populated, ranking 45th currently. With roughly 17 people per square mile, you'll always have plenty of room to spread your wings. The speed limits tend to be higher as a result (often 75 mph/120 kph) and aren't heavily enforced much of the time, which adds to one's sense of freedom.

Road trips across the state can be incredibly calming but may also leave you feeling quite isolated. It's not uncommon to drive for hours without seeing another car on the road, and sometimes the closest town will be 50 miles away. That's all great when solitude is what you're after, but it's also kind of unsettling in case of an emergency. Cell phone reception can be spotty, so it's important to have a back-up plan. For New Mexicans, that typically includes water, flares, an extra gallon of gas or two, a good spare tire, an emergency kit, and a blanket (New Mexico is considered 'high desert' country, which means days are hot while nights can be quite cold).

Also worthy of note is that nearly 75% of New Mexico's roads are unpaved. The state is dry so the risk of these dirt roads washing away is slim. That said, flash flooding can be an issue, especially during the summer monsoons. If you plan to explore the incredibly scenic back country, a high-clearance, four-wheel-drive vehicle is highly recommended, though not technically 'required'. Read on for tips on avoiding and surviving flash floods.

One more thing. New Mexico is one of four states that share a border with Mexico, albeit a small one. It isn't uncommon to run into random Border Patrol checkpoints on New Mexico's southern highways with cops and dogs looking for illegal aliens and drugs. US citizens usually skirt through just fine by flashing a driver's license. If you're visiting from outside the country, however, be sure to have your passport handy.

6. THERE'S AN APP FOR THAT

Below are the best travel apps to help you navigate your way around the state.

- ***New Mexico Travel Guide*** by Triposo—Excellent all-around app for finding famous sights, historical landmarks, entertainment venues, shopping centers, restaurants, and accommodation. Available for free at the App Store. Be sure to download the Triposo app as well or the information will slowly become dated.

- ***NM Roads***—This app is maintained by the state's Department of Transportation and is great if you plan to explore New Mexico by car. It provides updated information on road conditions, current weather, and construction delays, as well as live camera views. Available for free at the App Store and Google Play. Similar information can also be obtained by dialing 511 in-state.

- ***New Mexico State Parks***—A natural choice for nature lovers who want detailed information about New Mexico's state parks (including hours, directions, and current weather). Available for a modest fee at the App Store and Google Play.

7. XERISCAPING: NEW MEXICO'S APPROACH TO LANDSCAPING

One thing you'll notice in New Mexico is the frequent use of xeriscaping. Simply put, xeriscaping is landscaping that reduces or eliminates the need for irrigation water by taking advantage of native plants or rocks (or alternatively, by simply letting the weeds takeover, as is equally often the case). It's become quite popular in New Mexico where water is a precious commodity.

While ordering six tons of crushed rock to use as your front lawn might seem strange to the rest of the world, New Mexicans consider it the new norm. I'll admit that as a child, I did find it a bit odd watching my grandpa take a leaf blower to his green-colored rock lawn, but hey, xeriscaping certainly saves on the water bill and helps keep the state's limited water resources from being depleted too quickly.

8. TAKE A DEEP BREATH AND LATHER UP

Though perhaps hard to believe, Santa Fe is the highest capital city in the United States (and I'm not talking about the kind of chemically induced high other elevated capital cities like Denver are known for). Santa Fe sits at over 7,000 feet (2,134 meters). The air is thinner at high altitudes, so don't forget to take things slowly and breathe.

It's also important to understand that while July & August are technically the state's rainy season, New Mexico barely sees any significant precipitation during these months (or any other month for that matter). That means you'll be exposed to intense sun most of the year. Be sure to wear a hat, apply sunscreen generously, and drink lots of water. Water is one of the best preventative measures against altitude sickness and heat stroke. No joke.

9. DON'T GET CARRIED AWAY

Given New Mexico's dry climate, flash floods are always a concern. While most flooding occurs during the annual monsoon season (July & August), floods can happen anytime there is measurable, consistent precipitation.

Be sure to steer clear of slot canyons and arroyos (dry riverbeds) whenever rain is predicted, and NEVER wade or drive through floodwater, no matter how shallow it may look. 60% of all flood-related deaths in New Mexico are caused by people being swept away in their cars because they thought the water level looked low enough to drive through.

10. YOU MAY FIND THIS SHOCKING, BUT...

During the summer monsoon season (July & August), New Mexico experiences almost daily lightning storms. And get this, the state boasts more deaths by lightning than any other state in the country. That's not necessarily a statistic we're proud of, but an interesting bit of trivia nonetheless.

While the chance of getting struck by lightning is rare, even in the lightning-death capital of the US, it pays to pay attention to weather reports. Take lightning seriously and *bolt* for cover whenever storms are near. (Nice play on words, right? I'm on a [thunder] roll now.) Speaking of thunder, lightning storms are often accompanied by it, so remember the adage, 'When thunder roars, go indoors!'

Having said all that, if you really want to see lightning up close and personal, then you've come to the right place. New Mexican skies display some of the strongest, most brilliant lightning storms in the country.

27

11. AVOID BECOMING AN ACCIDENTAL TOURIST

While I'm not proud of this statistic, here's something else to be aware of when you're driving on our roads. New Mexico ranks first in the nation in alcohol-related automobile accidents. I suppose one consolation, if you can call it that, is that we only rank 25th in crash fatalities. Still….

Most of these accidents occur in the two northwest counties of McKinley & San Juan, but they can happen anywhere. Be sure to drive defensively on New Mexico's highways and avoid drinking and driving yourself. The statewide hotline for reporting drunk drivers is #394 (or #DUI).

12. CLOSE ENCOUNTERS OF THE DEADLY KIND

Remember those 'Stay on the Path' signs so common in National Parks and other outdoor tourist sites? Well, lean in closely and let me fill you in on a little secret—they're put there for a reason.

New Mexico has plenty of poisonous residents and you should be wary of all of them. Rattlesnakes, coral snakes and scorpions are all native to New Mexico, and they all have poisonous venom that can kill humans.

Scorpions are the deadliest. So deadly, in fact, they were chosen as my high school's mascot! (Shout out to Farmington High! Go, Scorps!) A sting from a scorpion immediately attacks the liver and will kill most humans in 24 hours if left untreated.

Coral snakes are the least deadly of the three. Only one human death from a coral snake bite has occurred since an anti-venom was released in 1967. Still, you don't want to be bitten by one, especially in the New Mexican outback where hospitals are few and far between.

Rattlesnakes can kill humans, too, though it takes a good two to three days for their venom to have that kind of effect. That doesn't mean you should seek them out or try to play with them. Tread lightly and stay on the path!

New Mexicans have a healthy respect for rattlesnakes and always have. For example, we don't typically eat them for dinner like next-door-neighbor Arizonans do, though you will find the odd restaurant that serves them up. Tastes just like chicken…seriously.

Instead of eating them, we revere them, as evidenced by The American International Rattlesnake

Museum in Albuquerque's Old Town. This worthwhile museum is on a mission to educate visitors about the myriad ways that rattlesnakes and other terrifying creatures have influenced the world for good. In the museum's own words, "myths are explored, phobias cured, and mysteries revealed."

Whether or not phobias are indeed cured, the museum does contain the largest collection of live snakes anywhere in the world, housing more slithering serpents than the National Zoo, the Bronx Zoo, the Philadelphia Zoo, the Denver Zoo, the San Francisco Zoo, and the San Diego Zoo combined! Heaven forbid these creatures ever break free! http://www.rattlesnakes.com/

13. PUT OUT OR GET OUT

You've heard of the four seasons, right? Well, New Mexico has five—spring, summer, fall, winter, and fire season.

New Mexico is a dry state, and fires in recent years have burned more than 150,000 acres of land and taken countless lives. Most wild fires are started by careless or deliberate humans, so please make sure to extinguish any fires you start before moving on.

14. SMOKEY BEAR: A STAR IS BORN

Speaking of forest fires, a mighty one raged in New Mexico's Lincoln National Forest back in 1950. Firefighters battling the blaze were shocked to find a three-month-old, five-pound black bear cub clinging to the top of a smoldering pine as the flames roared beneath him. His dramatic rescue drew national attention and Smokey Bear, as he came to be known, went on to become a living symbol of fire safety and wildlife conservation.

After touring the country, Smokey took up residence at the National Zoo in Washington, DC, where he entertained millions of visitors. The US Postal Service even gave him his own zip code due to the massive amounts of fan mail he received weekly. Following his death in 1976, the endearing bear's remains were returned to New Mexico where he was laid to rest in the small town of Capitan at the purpose-built Smokey Bear Historical Park and Interpretive Center—a small museum well worth visiting.

To date, Smokey Bear is the longest running and most successful public service ad campaign in United States history. The cartoon version of Smokey (which

31

predated the real bear by six years) still graces many 'Fire Danger' signs in America's National Parks and Forests and, according to a recent survey, is recognized by 80% of all Americans.

15. A NEW MEXICO STATE OF MIND

While we're on the topic of state symbols like Smokey Bear, let's explore a few others.

Most of the 50 states have a state motto, state song, state nickname, state bird, state flower, state tree, and state seal. Ever proud of our state, New Mexicans take things one step further…a lot further. Not only do we have all of the above, we also have a state air craft (*the hot air balloon*), state amphibian (*the New Mexico spadefoot*), state butterfly (*Sandia hairstreak*), state cookie (*biscochito*), state cowboy song (*Under The New Mexico Skies*), state fish (*Rio Grande cutthroat*), state folklorist (*Claude Stephenson*), state fossil (*Coelophysis*), state gem (*turquoise*), state guitar (*the New Mexico Sunrise*), state insect (*tarantula hawk wasp*), state mammal (*American black bear, just like Smokey*), state necklace (*the turquoise-laden squash blossom necklace*), state poem (*A Nueva Mexico, originally written in Spanish then translated into English*), state question (*more on that later*), state reptile (*the New Mexico whiptail*), and state vegetable (*the chile pepper, which some say is actually a fruit*). Really, New Mexico is a state of mind.

In the next three sections, I'll highlight only our state flower (*the yucca*), state bird (*the roadrunner*), and state flag (*a textile tribute to our Spanish and Native American heritage*).

16. THE LIFE-SAVING YUCCA PLANT

New Mexico students chose the yucca to be the state flower in 1927. Growing up in the northern half of the state, I always wondered, "Why the yucca?" (*pronounced yuh'-kuh*)…until I visited the state's southern half where the distinct-looking plant is prolific.

While some species of yucca look more like trees, the plant usually takes the form of a round bush with long, fibrous evergreen leaves and a flowering stem or two (or three) shooting straight up from the center.

Yuccas thrive in hot, dry, inhospitable climates and were a reliable source of food and clothing for indigenous peoples. Early American settlers jumped on the yucca bandwagon, too, and used the plant to feed themselves and their cattle during times of severe drought. The plant is, quite literally, a life saver.

Best places to see this unique flowering shrub? All over the southern third of the state.

17. YES, ROADRUNNERS ARE REAL!

Most people known about roadrunners ('mee-meep'!) from the Looney Toons cartoon series featuring Wile E. Coyote, a bound-and-determined bird eater who repeatedly tries to snag himself a roadrunner using comical contraptions, all of which miserably backfire (sometimes literally).

What some people may not know is that roadrunners are real birds, and no single bird is more 'in step' with New Mexicans. Able to fly (sort of) but preferring to run, the fastest roadrunner on record was clocked at 20 miles per hour. These little sprinters can often be seen scuttering along state highways and hiking paths—as long as you don't blink.

Weighing in at less than a pound, this small opportunistic omnivore has one of the bird world's most interesting defense mechanisms—its feet are shaped like Xs, which means that predators can't track which direction the bird is moving.

Today, in addition to being the state bird, the roadrunner has become the official mascot of the state's anti-littering 'Keep New Mexico Beautiful' campaign.

Best places to see them? Roadrunners can be found all over the state but blend in well with their natural surroundings. You'll just have to keep your eyes peeled. Or visit the Bitter Lake National Wildlife Refuge near Roswell, which posts bird sightings daily, including roadrunners.

18. OUR AWARD-WINNING FLAG

New Mexico's bold red and yellow banner came out on top with flying colors in a 2013 contest to find the best state flag in the country. USA Today organized the nationwide vote which ranked all 50 state flags according to voter preference. Go, New Mexico!

The proudly waving flag pays tribute to New Mexico's Native American and Spanish heritage and features a red-colored ancient Indian symbol on a bright yellow field. Red and yellow were the colors of Spain's Queen Isabella, who encouraged and financed her country's New World explorations. The Zia Pueblo, rumored to be one of the Seven Gold Cities of Cibola that brought Spanish explorers to New Mexico in the first place, is the source of the sun symbol.

Not only does the Zia sun symbol appear on New Mexico's state flag, it is also reflected in the design of the New Mexico State Capitol Building (which, as the only round state capital building in the US, looks like the Zia sun symbol when viewed from above). The Zia sun also features prominently on New Mexico state highway signs.

19. OUR PEOPLE: EVERYBODY IS SOMEBODY IN NEW MEXICO

New Mexico is one of two states where Hispanics outnumber all other ethnic groups. People of Hispanic origin make up more than half the state's residents while Native Americans account for 11%. When college friends of mine would visit for the first time, they commented, almost without exception, that they felt like they were in a foreign country. The ethnic diversity is one of the things I love most about New Mexico!

In step with our state slogan, 'Everybody is somebody in New Mexico,' New Mexicans are friendly, congenial, optimistic people. Whether you're in our largest cities or smallest towns, our national parks or 3.14 miles from the middle of nowhere (as comically named Pie Town, New Mexico, claims to be), you'll almost always be greeted and treated with kindness.

New Mexicans are also very down-to-earth. Even at the fanciest venues, it is not uncommon for attendees to be wearing jeans—fancied up with a bolo tie and silver belt buckle, of course. More on New Mexican fashion in section 22.

When it comes to photography, however, please note that many Native Americans do not like to have their picture taken, especially unsolicited. Never try to photograph them without their consent.

20. OUR LANGUAGES: A UNIQUE BLEND OF CULTURES AND VOCABULARIES

Nearly a third of New Mexico's residents speak Spanish as their primary language. That includes the direct descendants of Spanish conquistadors living in the isolated villages of Truchas, Chimayo, and Coyote who still speak a 16th-century form of Spanish found nowhere else in the world.

Indian tongues, especially Navajo and to a lesser degree Tewa, Tiwa, and Keres, are the first languages of choice for more than 5% of New Mexicans.

TIP: If you happen to be crossing from New Mexico to Arizona on US Highway 160, be sure to check out the cool state border sign written in both English and Navajo.

And here's an interesting tidbit. Because Navajo is such a complex, little-known language, Navajo 'code talkers' were employed to transmit top-secret messages during World War II, helping to bring about an end to the conflict.

Given the prominence of Spanish and Navajo, it should come as no surprise that 'loaner' words from each of these languages have become staples in New

Mexican English. The next section will introduce you to a few of them.

21. OUR CODE WORDS: HOW TO SPEAK LIKE A NATIVE

Below are a few 'New Mexican English' terms to help you speak like a native.

Adobe: No, we're not talking about the software giant, friends. In New Mexico, 'adobe' refers to our beautifully simple, environmentally sustainable architecture style that you'll see all over the state. It also refers to the mud plaster used in traditional adobe construction.

Arroyo: In New Mexico, this Spanish word for 'creek' or 'gulch' refers to a dry river bed prone to flash flooding. You'll pass over a lot of these as you drive across our state.

Casita: This Spanish word for 'little house' is used to describe cabins, condos, and other small dwellings in New Mexican English. It's also commonly used in restaurant names.

Chile: New Mexico's official spelling for chile peppers and anything made from them.

Christmas: The answer to New Mexico's state question when you want it both ways. Refer to section 33 for more details.

Duke City: New Mexico's largest city, Albuquerque, has been given many nicknames over the centuries—Querque, the Q, ABQ, and more recently Burque (from whence Burqueños hail). But none is as enduring as Duke City. The name dates to the early 1700s when King Philip of Spain allocated a parcel of land on the banks of the Rio Grande to an eager group of would-be colonists. The colony's governor named the new settlement after Spain's Duke of Alburquerque (no, that's not a typo). The first 'r' was eventually dropped from the name, but the Duke City moniker has remained ever since.

Fanta Se, The Fe or Hippietown: How Santa Fe residents often refer to their fair city.

Four Corners: The shortened version of Four Corners National Monument—the only place in the US where four state borders intersect. The term also refers to the entire area of northwest New Mexico, southwest Colorado, southeast Utah, and northeast Arizona. Farmington, as the largest city in the Four Corners region, is considered the main hub.

Howdy: The contracted version of "How do you do?" This expression is a common greeting across rural New Mexico.

Luminarias: Known as 'farolitos' in some parts of the state, luminarias are New Mexicans' most beloved Christmas decoration. These simple ornaments consist of brown paper bags filled with sand and a lighted candle. The state's most spectacular luminaria display takes place at San Juan College in Farmington the first Saturday in December.

The Pit: The semi-underground basketball court where the University of New Mexico Lobos play and where Lobos fans demonstrate why they're considered some of the loudest and the proudest in the country.

The Rez: How New Mexicans' refer to the state's Indian lands, especially the Navajo Nation in the northwest corner of the state, because, you know, 'reservation' just takes too long to say.

Ristras: Essentially a string of chile peppers. Ristras originated as a method of drying and preserving pepper pods but have evolved into a favorite New Mexican decoration.

T or C: Few alive today will remember the interactive 1940s game show called 'Truth Or

Consequences' that was broadcast across the country by radio. To celebrate the show's 10th anniversary in 1950, the host dared any town in the US to change its name to match that of the show. The citizens of Hot Springs, New Mexico, did just that, voting 1,294 to 295 to officially change their name to Truth or Consequences ('T or C' for short).

Tamalewood: The nickname for New Mexico's independent film industry.

Taos: Incorrectly pronouncing the name of this art town/pueblo is a dead giveaway that you're not a native. 'Tous' is the correct pronunciation, kind of like 'house' with a 't'.

Topes: The slang term for New Mexico's minor league baseball team, the Albuquerque Isotopes.

Trailer: How most New Mexicans refer to mobile homes, in which 20% of the state's residents live.

Vigas: The Spanish word for 'rafters' that refers to rough-hewn wooden beams that run the length of indoor ceilings and often extend to the exterior of New Mexican homes.

Zozobra: Also known as 'Old Man Gloom', the Zozobra is a 50-foot tall marionette that's stuffed with misfortune and set ablaze each September at the start of Santa Fe's annual Fiesta. Refer to section 46 on Festivals for more details.

22. OUR CLOTHING: WARDROBE ESSENTIALS FOR FASHIONISTAS

New Mexicans have a unique style of dress, reflective of both our Western and Native American heritage. Below are the most prominent clothing items you're most likely to encounter during a visit to our fair state.

Bolo Tie

A bolo tie is a type of necktie typically associated with Western wear. It consists of a braided leather cord capped with silver tips that's fastened together with an ornamental clip called an aglet. The bolo tie was made New Mexico's official state neckwear in 1987 and its official state tie in 2007. Bolos are worn throughout New Mexico by men and women and can be considered both dressy and smart-casual depending on the situation.

Sterling Silver Belt Buckles

The native tribes of the American Southwest have been making silver belt buckles since silversmithing was first introduced to them in the 1850s. Many belt buckles are laden with turquoise stone, and the bigger the buckle and more intricate the design, the better.

Turquoise Jewelry

Most of the turquoise mined in the US comes from Arizona, Nevada, and New Mexico. The blue-green, semi-precious stone's accessibility is but one of many reasons the Navajo use it to make jewelry. Heck, we love it so much in New Mexico, our license plates are even turquoise-colored.

The Navajo consider the stone a living mineral, partly because of its color-changing abilities, and Navajo medicine men have used it for centuries to identify and cure a variety of ailments. According to jewelry makers, there's no better way to harness the stone's enlightening and enabling power than to adorn one's body with it.

Extras

Add fashion and flare to your bolo tie, belt buckle, and turquoise jewelry by donning a pair of cowboy boots (preferably black) and a cowboy hat (also preferably black). Many New Mexicans do. You'll look sharp by New Mexican standards wherever you go.

23. DON'T FAKE IT: HOW TO MAKE SURE TURQUOISE JEWELRY IS REAL

Tourists looking to purchase turquoise jewelry should be wary of fakes. Counterfeit stones do a great disservice to the history, cultural importance, and sacred nature of turquoise, as well as the centuries-old craft and care surrounding it.

To ensure you aren't buying a fake, follow these three simple rules:

1) Purchase turquoise jewelry from a certified Navajo jeweler.

2) Look for black or white veins or blotches in the stone (referred to as the matrix). While not all 'real' turquoise has a matrix, most of it does.

3) If it looks suspicious, ask the seller if you can take a flame to it (cigarette lighters are the most common source). Most will say yes if the stone is authentic. The smelly resin often used as a bonding agent in manufactured or reconstituted turquoise will blacken and smell bad when exposed to an open flame.

24. OUR INDIAN TRIBES

New Mexicans don't often refer to Native Americans the politically correct way. The term 'Indian' is still quite common and seldom considered offensive, though there are exceptions. If you haven't noticed already, I use 'Indian' and 'Native American' interchangeably in this book.

Twenty-three Native American tribes call New Mexico home—nineteen Pueblo clusters, three Apache tribes, and the granddaddy of them all, the Navajo Nation.

Each tribe is technically its own sovereign nation with its own unique relationship to federal and state governments. Likewise, the land allocated to them by the United States Department of the Interior (commonly referred to as 'reservations' because the land is *reserved* for them), qualifies as a semi-independent nation state. More on that in a bit.

The Navajo

The Navajo are the state's largest tribe by population and the second largest federally recognized tribe in the country. There are more than 350,000 registered Navajos, whose territory spans three states (New Mexico, Arizona, Utah). About one-third live in New Mexico.

The Navajo reservation is also the largest in the country and was expanded as recently as 2016. Yes, the Navajo Nation is larger than ten individual US states, meaning it's BIG.

The Apache

Despite their comparatively small number, the Apache have always been a force to be reckoned with. Comprised of several sub-tribes, they collectively fought the Spanish and Mexicans for centuries. Their men were feared for their guerilla-like war tactics while their women were renowned for their ability to quickly assemble and tear down the tribe's tent-like housing structures called wickiups. Today there are a total of 30,000 registered Apaches living in New Mexico, Arizona, and Oklahoma.

The Pueblo

The term 'Pueblo' has a dual meaning. It originally referred to Native American groups in the American Southwest that were bound together by common linguistic, agricultural, and religious practices. Later, the Spanish expanded its definition by using it to refer to the multi-story adobe villages in which they found the Pueblos living. 'Pueblo' means 'village' in Spanish, so the double entendre is perfectly justifiable.

There are currently 19 pueblos, or towns, in New Mexico, including what is perhaps the most iconic— the Taos Pueblo in the north-central part of the state. Those that are still inhabited have been lived in for centuries. Most allow visitors.

25. WHY DO INDIAN RESERVATIONS LOOK LIKE THIRD WORLD COUNTRIES?

New Mexico is a poor state, and that will become painfully evident as you drive across The Land of Enchantment (our official nickname since 1990). 20% of New Mexicans live in mobile homes (you know, the kind you park in one spot and leave there for a while).

And then there are the Indian reservations, which, as I mentioned previously, New Mexicans rarely refer to the politically correct way. Even 'reservation' takes too long to say and is often abbreviated as simply 'the Rez'.

Having grown up just a few miles from the country's largest Indian reservation, what seems perfectly normal to me is often deemed shocking, even scandalous, by visitors. Crudely built shanties free of building code restrictions dot the reservation landscape while mobile homes and government-built houses of identical shape, color, and size begin to appear the closer one gets to reservation towns, all in the shadows of flashy casinos and uber-modern medical facilities.

By today's definition, third world countries are nations with high mortality rates, low literacy rates, widespread poverty, and an economic structure that does not allow for financial mobility. New Mexico's Indian Reservations fit that bill on all counts. With all of today's focus on America's richest 1%, a look at America's Indian reservations, where many of the nation's poorest 1% live, would be more instructive.

No, alcoholism and high employment aren't the cause of all this. They're the symptoms—symptoms of a much bigger phenomenon that is often touted as being core to the Native Americans' culture and way of life. Let me explain.

26. THE CURSE OF COMMUNAL LAND

Navajo reservation land is owned communally. While this seems in line with what has been widely flaunted as a fundamental Native American belief (i.e., that land cannot be owned and therefore must be mutually respected and shared), the byproduct of this philosophy is actually quite different. It's what economists call 'the tragedy of the commons'.

Because all reservation land is communal (in other words, owned by everyone in the tribe), it is essentially owned by no one (at least in the sense that residents can never obtain a title to the land on which their residence sits). Why, then, would you invest in a nice home or try to create a beautiful yard if the tribal government could ask you to relocate at any given moment? You wouldn't.

Prosperity is built on individual property rights, which most reservations simply don't offer. With no land ownership, it is difficult for reservation dwellers to establish a line of credit or build any equity. Because they own very few things of value to use as collateral for a loan and have no mortgage payments to prove their credit-worthiness, they tend to spend their government checks on flashy pick-up trucks, jewelry, and satellite TV rather than investing in their future.

One more nail in the economic coffin is the lack of private investment on Indian reservations. Most private business investors, with the exception of those running trading posts, convenience stores, or big-brand fast-food restaurants, won't touch reservations with a ten-foot totem pole due to tricky tribal laws and immature building codes. Even casinos have failed to produce the benefits they so often promised pre-construction. Until reservations can become part of the national, and even global, economies, they will likely remain impoverished.

27. FREEDOM, OPPORTUNITY OR BONDAGE WITH EASE? YOU PICK.

Fortunately, living on the reservation is a lifestyle choice for present-day American Indians. Like all US citizens, Native Americans can live and work wherever they like, and plenty do. As many as 50% leave the reservations seeking education and employment opportunities. Others are enticed by the 'reservation easy life' where the promise of 'free' housing, 'free' medical care, low to non-existent taxes, and monthly government checks to spend as they please allure many. It's a lifestyle choice, really.

Some may argue I've oversimplified things. In a sense, they're right. The situation on America's reservations is far more complex than I could possibly explain in a few paragraphs. I haven't even touched on how tribal and federal government agencies enable and encourage it all. I have simply shared a few things I've learned and experienced firsthand growing up near the country's largest 'Rez'. We'll leave it at this for now.

28. TOP 5 PLACES TO EXPERIENCE NATIVE AMERICAN CULTURE

Despite the poverty on our reservations, New Mexico has a rich, deep-rooted Native American heritage that spans several millennia. With 23 tribes, 19 pueblos, and a highly visible Native American population that ranks fourth in the nation, New Mexico offers a wealth of Indian-related experiences. Below are my Top 5 recommendations for those looking to experience Native American culture.

Please note that while all of the pueblos I've listed do welcome visitors, many have strict rules about photography. You wouldn't want strangers wandering about taking random pictures of you or your house now, would you?

Acoma Pueblo (near Grants) XXX

In Keres, the language spoken by Acoma Pueblo Indians, the word 'acoma' means 'the place that always was'—a fitting name for a pueblo that's regarded as the oldest continuously inhabited community in the United States.

The pueblo itself sits atop a 370-feet high mesa. A mere 13 families live in the pueblo today, serving as caretakers and tour guides of the pueblo and its newly built Cultural Center, which houses a top-notch pottery museum, gift shop, and café serving both Acoma and New Mexican fare.

To get here, take exit 102 off I-40 (45 miles west of Albuquerque) and travel 12 miles south.

Chaco Culture National Historical Park (near Farmington)

The veritable jewel of New Mexico's Native American legacy, hard-to-reach Chaco Canyon houses a network of pueblos and hiking trails. Visitors can get up close and personal with the pueblos' decorative T-shaped doorways, still-in-tact living quarters, ancient stone stairways, and petroglyphs, all of which date to as early as A.D. 850. The site has also been designated an International Dark Sky Park, which means it's an excellent place for star-gazing.

To get here from the north, follow County Road 7900 which is located three miles southeast of Nageezi off US Highway 550. The 21-mile road (eight miles of which are paved) leads to the site. Note that the last four and a half miles before entering the park are extremely rough. Entry roads from the south are even more rough and often impassable.

Indian Pueblo Cultural Center (Albuquerque)

This modern museum is owned and operated by the 19 Indian Pueblos that call New Mexico home. Offering an extensive collection of Pueblo pottery, baskets, jewelry, and art, as well as regular dance shows, the Center is dedicated to educating visitors about Pueblo culture, history, art, and modern-day accomplishments while promoting established and emerging Pueblo artists. Likewise, the Pueblo Harvest Café gives visitors an opportunity to sample indigenous cuisine. The Center makes a great stopping point before exploring the actual pueblos.

https://www.indianpueblo.org/

Taos Pueblo (Taos)

According to archaeologists, Puebloans lived in this multistory adobe complex long before Columbus arrived in the Americas. The compound's present-day structures were built between A.D. 1000 and 1450, making this pueblo one of the oldest continuously inhabited communities in the country. 150 residents live there today, much as their ancestors did centuries ago without the benefits of electricity, running water or air-conditioning.

The Pueblo, located at 120 Veterans Highway just outside Taos, can be visited for a fee. An extra charge is applied for non-commercial and commercial cameras, including phones. http://taospueblo.com/

Zuni Pueblo (near Gallup)

Nestled in a tranquil valley surrounded by sandstone mesas, the Zuni Pueblo is famous for many reasons: (1) it's the largest of New Mexico's 19 pueblos; (2) it's the first place the Spanish came looking for gold in the mid-1500s; and (3) it's home to some of the best pottery and jewelry artists in the state. Roughly 6,500 Zuni Pueblo live in the village, which is open to visitors year-round.

Before visiting the pueblo itself, be sure to stop at the helpful Visitor & Arts Center. Friendly staff will help you know exactly which sites can be visited and photographed (for a fee).

To reach the Pueblo from I-40, take Route 602 south from Gallup then turn west on Route 53.

29. TOP 5 PLACES TO BUY NATIVE AMERICAN SOUVENIRS

Native Americans have been making art for centuries. If you want to know the piece of art you purchase is authentic (and you'd like the ability to bargain), it's best to go to the artists themselves. Here are my Top 5 recommended places for viewing and purchasing Native American art.

Santa Fe Indian Art Market (Santa Fe)

The Santa Fe Indian Art Market is a juried art show that takes place twice a year—once in the summer (mid-August) and again in the winter (December). The summer market is definitely the granddaddy of the two, occupying Santa Fe's central Plaza and spilling into surrounding streets and local galleries. Prices at this art fair tend to be non-negotiable, though vendors are more willing to bargain toward the end of the show. http://swaia.org/

Palace of the Governors (Santa Fe)

The Palace of the Governors is located on the north side of the Plaza in the heart of Santa Fe. Sellers of Native American jewelry, pottery, rugs, sand paintings, and other types of art line the sidewalk in front of the Palace from morn until eve. In order to set up shop at this prime location, a vendor must be a licensed Native American, his or her merchandise must be original and handmade, and he or she must be the artist or closely related to the artist. The vendors change daily so if you see something you like, buy it, as it may not be there the next day. Prices are negotiable and certificates of authenticity accompany most purchases.
http://www.palaceofthegovernors.org

Four Corners National Monument (near Shiprock)

Four Corners National Monument is a great place to go for Native American souvenirs, especially during the height of the tourist season (late May to early September).

Permanent booths encircle the Monument and artists are typically there from mid-morning to early evening. While some souvenirs are a bit kitschy, most jewelry will come with a certificate of authenticity and most sand paintings will be signed by the artist. Expect to pay roughly two-thirds of the asking price.

Gallup Native Arts Market (Gallup)

The Native Arts Market in downtown Gallup took flight in 2017 and, with multifaceted support from both the city and local tribes, is destined to become one of the region's largest. The Market takes place over three days in early August and offers a treasure trove of Native American souvenirs.
https://www.gallupnativeartsmarket.org/

Roadside Stands (Toadlena)

As you weave your way across northwestern New Mexico, be sure to stop in the town that's known for its hand-woven wool rugs. Here you'll be able to watch Native American artists wind and twist naturally-dyed sheep's wool into intricate shapes and symbols—a labor-intensive process that will help you understand why Navajo rugs are so expensive.

HINT: Purchase rugs and other Native American souvenirs from the roadside stands that abound in high season. You'll find things much cheaper there than in local Trading Posts.

30. TOP 5 PLACES TO SEE PETROGLYPHS

New Mexico is an archaeologist's dream, and those looking to channel their inner 'Indiana Jones' will find a plethora of postcard-worthy petroglyph sites. Below are my Top 5 recommendations.

Mesa Prieta (near Espanola)

Boasting more than 75,000 petroglyphs, the 13-mile Mesa Prieta ('dark table' in English) is easily the state's largest repository of ancient stone carvings. And because it's still an active archaeological site, new discoveries of all kinds are constantly being made. Please note the Petroglyph Preserve sits on private land and is closed on Sundays, Mondays, and in the winter. Non-profit public and private tours, each lasting about two hours, must be booked in advance. No children under 10, pets, or commercial

photography allowed.
http://www.mesaprietapetroglyphs.org

Cieneguilla Petroglyph Site (near Santa Fe)

Think graffiti is a recent phenomenon? Think again. La Cieneguilla contains one of the most concentrated collections of rock art in New Mexico, and in the Western United States, for that matter. The site is a short distance from the Santa Fe airport and I-25, which is both good and bad. Good because it's easily accessible, and bad because it's easily accessible. Sadly, the irreplaceable etchings are often used for target practice by paintballers and wanna-be marksmen. Please tread lightly if you come.

From NM 599, travel 3.3. miles west on Paseo Real to the gravel parking lot and hiking trail head. It's about an 8-minute walk down a well-marked trail to reach the petroglyph site.

Crow Canyon Petroglyphs (near Farmington)

Crow Canyon is the hidden gem of my hometown community. This remote and relatively unknown petroglyph site is said to contain the most extensive collection of Navajo rock art anywhere in the Southwest, much of which is clear, vibrant, and at eye level (no scrambling required). Be advised the site isn't the easiest to get to and feels awfully remote, despite being close to Farmington and situated on BLM land with decent signage. Plan accordingly.

To get there, take County Road 4450 east from US Highway 64 for about 19 miles. Even though County Road 4450 is a reasonably maintained dirt road, the area is prone to flash flooding. Do not come here if rain is forecast.

Three Rivers Petroglyph Site (near Tularosa)

Lurking in the shadows of one of New Mexico's top attractions (White Sands National Monument), poor Three Rivers is often overlooked. That's a shame, since the site is easily accessible and contains over 21,000 petroglyphs, some of which were carved as early as A.D. 200.

To get to Three Rivers, follow US Highway 54 north from Tularosa for 17 miles. Take a right on Three Rivers Road (also known as Otero County Road B30) and continue on for just over five miles to the large parking lot. A daily entrance fee of $5 per vehicle is charged (free if you have a National Parks pass) and knowledgeable park rangers are available to answer questions. There is also a covered shelter at the trailhead in the event of rain (rare) or severe heat (likely).

Bandelier National Monument (near Los Alamos)

Bandelier is one of those awesome places that allows you to kill two bucket-list birds with one stone (sandstone, that is). Petroglyphs and dwelling places were both carved into the sandstone cliffs by humans who lived at Bandelier at least 11,000 years ago. Petroglyphs are more limited here, but again it's 2-for-1.

Plan to spend at least half a day to fully appreciate the Visitors Center and the cliff dwellings—longer if you plan to hike the back country. Guided, hour-long ranger tours leave the Visitors Center in summer months. All other tours are self-guided. Come in the late afternoon on an off-season day to enjoy the solitude.

From Los Alamos, take NM Highway 501 or 502 to NM Highway 4 and follow the signs to the entrance.

31. OUR FOOD: IT'S CALLED 'NEW MEX', NOT 'TEX MEX'

While many states have a signature crop or dish (think Georgia peaches, Texas barbecue, Idaho potatoes, Maine lobster, Wisconsin cheese, etc.), New Mexico has its own signature *cuisine*—a tasty blend of Native American, Spanish, and Mexican cooking styles that's been adapted and refined over 400 years. Its main distinguishing factor is the prominent use of chiles (and no, that's not a typo).

32. CHILE OR CHILI?

New Mexicans are very proud of their chile, and justifiable so. The state produces more than 60% of all chile peppers sold in the US. We literally put chiles in or on everything, including eggs, pizza, sandwiches, burgers, mac-n-cheese, meatballs, hummus, popcorn, waffles, wine, lemonade, and even milkshakes (yes, you read that right—don't knock it 'til you try it).

I remember when my youngest sister brought her out-of-state fiancé home to meet the family. Two days into his visit, my future brother-in-law asked, "Is there any chance we could have just one meal without green chiles?" Yes, chiles are a way of life in New

63

Mexico. I can't imagine life without them. Perhaps that's why New Mexicans insist on spelling 'chile' OUR WAY!

For New Mexicans, 'chile' refers not to the South American country but to any type of green or red pepper that grows in the state. This spelling dates to the arrival of the Spanish in the 1500s and was formalized as the state's official spelling in 1983.

'Chili,' on the other hand, refers to 'chili con carne'—a soupy blend of ground beef, beans, and tomato paste that means 'chili with meat' in Spanish.

33. RED OR GREEN?

New Mexico is the only state in the country with an official state question: Red or Green? The question refers to the type of chile sauce a person likes best. Some prefer red, others prefer green, and then there are those like me who simply can't decide. Not to worry. If you'd like to have both, just request 'Christmas', which means you want red chile on one side of your dish and green chile on the other. Yes, in New Mexico, we don't just celebrate Christmas. We order it, eat it, and rejoice in it on an almost daily basis!

It's important to note that red chile sauce is typically beef-based while green chile sauce is often pork-based. There are very few vegetarian versions, though some restaurants have started to offer meat-free sauce options.

Green chiles are typically fire-roasted to soften the peel, allowing it to be removed. Red chiles, on the other hand, are usually dried, ground into powder, then rehydrated to create a delicious sauce.

And while we're on the topic, let me put to rest a widely circulated rumor. Green chiles are NOT hotter than red ones. While redder chiles are assumed to be milder and greener chiles are supposedly spicier, the level of heat actually depends on how ripe the chile is, regardless of color. In layman's terms, the longer the chile matures on the vine, the hotter it will be when it's served up. Don't let the color fool you!

34. TOP 5 NEW MEXICAN FOODS YOU HAVE TO TRY

New Mexico offers a wealth of interesting dishes you won't find anywhere else. Below are my Top 5 recommendations, though there are many, many more to try.

Carne Adovada

Ever wonder what you'd get if you mixed crushed red chiles, pureed onions, and a host of other spices, then lathered the mouth-watering mix over pork and let it simmer for 24 hours? Carne adovada is the correct answer. And carne adovada is, quite simply, a pork-lovers paradise.

For those who prefer a soup to sauce, try posole—a hearty New Mexico-style gumbo made with similar ingredients (pork, red chiles) and hominy (dried maize kernels from which the bran and germ have been removed).

Best place to try some? Sadie's of New Mexico in Albuquerque. http://www.sadiesofnewmexico.com/

Chile relleno

Even though chile rellenos originated in Old Mexico, New Mexicans have perfected them. A chile relleno, which means 'stuffed chile' in Spanish, is essentially a green chile pepper stuffed with Oaxaca cheese (a stringy white cheese from Mexico), dipped in egg batter, then deep fried. Avoid this if you're counting calories.

Best place to try one? Los Hermanitos in Farmington. http://www.loshermanitos.com/

Chimichangas

A New Mexican invention, the chimichanga is essentially a deep-fried burrito. This tasty bit of fried paradise is often smothered with chile sauce (usually red) then topped with cheese, lettuce, sour cream, and tomatoes. Like its cousins—flautas and taquitos—the chimichanga can be eaten with a fork or with fingers.

Best place to try one? My mom's house. But since you probably won't be invited anytime soon, head to Federico's Mexican Food with three locations in Albuquerque. https://federicosmexicanfood.com/

Frito Pies

The New Mexican capital city of Santa Fe and the entire state of Texas both claim to have invented the Frito pie. Who's right? Who knows? Both have substantial documentation to prove their point. I say, who cares? And you won't care either once you've taken a bite of these crispy, salty corn chips smothered with chili con carne then topped with grated cheese. Best eaten with a fork and a spoon so as not to miss a morsel.

Best place to try one? Head to the El Parasol food truck restaurant in Espanola if you want some of the best.

Sopapillas

Sopapillas are unique to New Mexico and were first made in Albuquerque over 200 years ago. They are essentially fluffy, flaky, hollow puff pastries…and the bigger, the better. While sopapillas are traditionally served as either a side or dessert, they can also be a main course when stuffed with beans, beef, cheese and, of course, chile sauce.

Best place to try some? It's hard to find any bigger, fluffier or flakier than those at Los Hermanitos in Farmington. www.loshermanitos.com

35. TOP 5 NATIVE AMERICAN FOODS YOU HAVE TO TRY

Indigenous cuisine in New Mexico is heavily influenced by traditional crops and ancestral cooking methods. The Pueblo Indians were farmers, growing several varieties of corn, squash, and beans. The Navajo became farmers as well, but also herded sheep and goats. You'll notice a prominent use of corn, beans, mutton, and lard in most all Native dishes. Here are my Top 5 recommendations.

Blue Corn anything

Maize has been a staple in the diet of Southwest American Indians for centuries and blue corn, with its strong nutty flavor, is an essential ingredient in New Mexican cuisine. It is commonly used to make tortillas, pancakes, muffins, cornbread, corn chips, porridge, and even batter for onion rings and other fried foods like chile rellenos.

Best place to try it? It's hard to beat the taste and variety of blue corn options available at the Pueblo Harvest in Albuquerque.
https://www.puebloharvestcafe.com/

Fry Bread

Fry bread is, quite simply, flattened dough fried in oil, shortening, or lard. Though made with simple ingredients, it is absolutely delicious and a well-loved treat that is routinely sold at high school sporting events and festivals, especially in the northwest part of the state. Fry bread can be eaten plain or topped with cinnamon sugar, powdered sugar, honey, jam or chocolate.

Best place to try it? Any of the food trailers at Four Corners National Monument.

Horno Bread

Pronounced with a silent 'h' like the words 'or' and 'no' together, hornos are beehive-shaped adobe ovens traditionally used by the Pueblo Indians of New Mexico and Arizona. The ingredients for horno bread are simple and straightforward. It's the baking process that makes it special. There is nothing quite like fresh-baked bread served hot from a clay oven.

Best place to try it? The Taos Pueblo just outside Taos or take a class and make your own at The Feasting Place. http://www.thefeastingplace.com/

Mutton Stew

Spanish explorers in the 1600s introduced the Navajo to 'la raza churra', a hardy breed of sheep from Spain that sparked a radical lifestyle change for the tribe. Ever since, sheep have been a primary source of meat to the Navajos (hence, the prominence of mutton in their diet). Common ingredients in mutton stew (besides sheep meat) include potatoes, carrots, squash, corn, celery, and onions. It's traditionally served with fry bread.

Best place to try it? Any of the food trucks at the Shiprock Flea Market. http://local-fleamarkets.com/ShiprockNewMexicoFleaMarket

Navajo Tacos

Another take on fry bread is the delectable, Native American-inspired Navajo taco. Native Americans themselves refer to the dish as a 'Navajo taco' or 'Indian taco', so don't feel discriminatory calling it that. The tacos are built on fry bread, piled high with saucy beans (often mixed with ground beef), smothered in chile sauce, then topped with lettuce, cheese, tomatoes, and sour cream.

Best place to try one? If you're in northern New Mexico, any of the food trailers at Four Corners

National Monument. If you're in the southern part of the state, try the Largo Café on US Highway 16 in Quemado.

36. TOP 5 NEW MEXICAN SWEET-TOOTH SATISFIERS

Biscochito

To date, New Mexico is one of only two US states with an official state cookie. Massachusetts is the other, though Michigan did introduce legislation in 2004 to become the third (that legislation hasn't been 'officially' adopted yet). The biscochito originated in Spain and was introduced to New Mexico by Spanish settlers. If you like black licorice and other anise-flavored treats, you'll love these.

Cactus candy

Prickly pear cacti grow throughout New Mexico. The plant flowers annually and the nectar that's extracted from the flower is sugared-up and turned into jelly-like candy, which is then coated with a layer of sugar.

Churros

Churros may be a decidedly Mexican dessert but remember, New Mexican cuisine is a unique blend of Mexican, Spanish, and Native American foods. These long, fried donut sticks are rolled in a mix of cinnamon and sugar to create a tasty, fun-to-eat treat that can be dipped or eaten plain. Sometimes they even come filled with vanilla cream or caramel.

Fried Ice Cream

Fried ice cream is a frozen ball of vanilla ice cream that's breaded with corn flakes, nuts, or graham cracker crumbles, cinnamon and egg whites then quickly deep-fried, thus creating a caramelized, crispy outer shell with a solid ice cream center. While its origins are debated (some say Chicago, some say Philadelphia, some say Japan), New Mexicans have once again perfected the dish. You'll find this delicious dessert in any good New Mexican restaurant.

Sopapillas

Yep, they're not just for dinner. Sopapillas make a great dessert, especially when they're coated with powdered sugar, cinnamon, or honey then served with vanilla ice cream.

37. TOP 5 RESTAURANTS THAT OFFER A TRULY NEW MEXICAN EXPERIENCE

If you haven't gathered by now, food is a big part of New Mexican culture. Anyone seeking a truly New Mexican culinary experience with a bit of history thrown in will want to check out these restaurants below. All are personal favorites.

66 Diner (Albuquerque)

Step inside the 66 Diner and you'll feel as though you've traveled back in time. Deemed 'futuristic' in its heyday, this now-retro, neon-clad restaurant celebrates New Mexico's Route 66 history like no other, complete with all the requisite 1950s classics like jukeboxes, checkered countertops, and a soda fountain. Its milkshakes have been voted New Mexico's best. Come at night to admire the neon. http://www.66diner.com

Rancho de Chimayo (Chimayo)

Decorated with dangling chile ristras on the outside and an eclectic hodge podge of 'whatever I feel like' on the inside, Rancho de Chimayo serves up a tasty range of New Mexican staples like chile rellenos, blue corn enchiladas, house-made refried beans and Spanish rice, as well as pinon coffee and prickly pear (cactus) frozen lemonade to wash it all down. http://www.ranchodechimayo.com/

Sparky's Burgers (Hatch)

Live music, wood-fired barbecue, handcrafted coffees, and made-from-scratch green chile cheeseburgers pretty much sum up Sparky's in a nutshell. You can't miss its '50s-style exterior. Of course, being located in the Green Chile Capital of the World, almost everything at Sparky's is served up with a splash of locally harvested green chile, guaranteed to make your taste buds dance and sing. The only drawback to Sparky's is that the restaurant is closed Monday through Wednesday. Plan your visit to Hatch accordingly. www.sparkysburgers.com

Pueblo Harvest (Albuquerque)

If it's Native American fare you're craving, then Pueblo Harvest is the place for you! For breakfast, try the blue corn pancakes or blue corn porridge. Then again, if you really want a taste of New Mexico, you might prefer the blue corn chicken waffle, which consists of a blue corn-crusted chicken breast, a red chile waffle, and green chile maple syrup. For lunch and dinner, try the blue corn enchiladas, blue corn-crusted chile relleno, or Indian taco served on spongy fry bread with a side of blue corn onion rings. Mutton stew is also served. www.puebloharvestcafe.com

Tia Sophia's (Santa Fe)

Credited with giving the world its first official breakfast burrito back in 1975, Tia Sophia's still serves up tortilla-wrapped, chile-drenched scrambled eggs. According to the New Mexico Department of Tourism, an official breakfast burrito must include at least three key ingredients: (1) scrambled eggs; (2) a tortilla; and (3) New Mexico chile in one form or another. Beans, meat, cheese, hash brown potatoes, sour cream, and avocados are all acceptable extras. Other New Mexican staples like sopapillas (stuffed and plain), chile rellenos, posole, and blue corn enchiladas also splatter the menu. The restaurant proudly serves breakfast and lunch but is closed for dinner. https://www.tiasophias.com

BONUS: I'd be remiss if I didn't mention Blake's Lotaburger, a home-grown New Mexican quick-serve chain that's been serving up burgers and fries since 1952. Blake's repeatedly wins state-wide and local awards for the best green chile cheeseburger, best breakfast burrito, and best milkshakes. There are 70 locations across the state and a few in Texas and Arizona, too. https://www.lotaburger.com/

38. TOP 5 DRINKS TO WASH IT ALL DOWN

Once you've sampled our tasty cuisine, you'll want to wash it all down with one of our five signature drinks.

Water

We're high and dry, folks, and nothing sucks moisture out of your body like altitude and dry air. Definitely drink more water while you're in New Mexico, and not just after meals. It's one of the best ways to combat dehydration (*duh!*) and altitude sickness (*you don't say?*).

Best place to try it? Judges recently rated Albuquerque's water the best in the state based on clarity, odor, feel, and taste.

Green Chile Wine

Jesus may have turned water into wine at the wedding feast of Canaan (John 2:1-11), but New Mexicans would never want to waste a precious drop of the life-giving liquid by transforming it into something else. And they don't have to. New Mexico's climate is perfect for growing grapes and, by extension, producing wine. As many as fifty wineries are scattered across the state. Wine-bibbers should be sure to try New Mexico's own chile wine, made by blending white wine with New Mexican red or green chiles. Green is the most popular.

Best place to try it? Any St. Clair Bistro statewide or the St. Clair Winery & Tasting Room in Deming. https://www.stclairwinery.com

Green Chile Lemonade

While it may sound strange, this New Mexican classic becomes increasingly addictive with each sip. That's because the chiles help tone down the lemonade's bitterness while amplifying its sweetness. As we say in The Land of Enchantment, don't knock it 'til you try it!

Best place to try it? Sparky's Burgers in Hatch. http://www.sparkysburgers.com/

Green Chile Milkshake

The recipe is simple. Whip 20 ounces of soft-serve ice cream with a quarter cup of green chiles (roasted, peeled, and diced, of course) then serve cold. As with green chile lemonade, the chiles enhance the sweetness of the ice cream. It's the ultimate sweet-'n'-spicy treat.

Best place to try it? Sparky's Burgers in Hatch. http://www.sparkysburgers.com/

Pinon Coffee

Another New Mexican classic, pinon coffee is a high-altitude, multi-bean blend fused together with the edible pine nuts that flourish in New Mexico's high desert clime. Though not a coffee drinker myself, I'm told the aroma is similar to coffees infused with chicory or hazel nut.

Best place to try it? The crazy-busy Owl Café in Albuquerque. You can't miss it, since the building's exterior is shaped like an owl.
http://www.owlcafealbuquerque.com

39. TOP 5 PLACES TO STAY FOR A TRULY NEW MEXICAN EXPERIENCE

Inn & Spa at Loretto (Santa Fe)

The 'Inn' is a boutique gem in the heart of Santa Fe whose list of awards and accolades is as impressive as it is endless. Situated one block from Santa Fe's historic Plaza and right next door to the mystical Loretto chapel, the Inn & Spa at Loretto looks like a replica of the Taos Pueblo, making it one of the most photographed buildings in Santa Fe. It's the perfect place to experience Southwest hospitality and rich Santa Fe style. https://www.hotelloretto.com/

Earthship Rentals (near Taos)

Driving across northern New Mexico on Highway 64, you'll pass the world's first-ever Earthship community near Taos. You can't miss it, since the 'ships' look like something straight out of a sci-fi novel.

Earthships are self-contained, off-the-grid dwellings made of natural and recycled materials. Electricity is generated using solar and wind power; water is harvested from rain, snow, and condensation; interior temperatures are comfortably maintained by large glass windows and dirt-rammed rubber tire walls. It's really quite ingenious.

While the Taos Earthship Community consists mostly of private residences, the Earthship Biotecture main office does rent out select units to curious travelers. Privately-owned Earthships have also begun cropping up on vacation rental sites like VRBO and Airbnb. https://www.earthshipglobal.com/

Kokopelli Cave (near Farmington)

In Native American culture, Kokopelli is a flute-playing fertility god that is both playful and mischievous. In this sense, Farmington's Kokopelli Cave certainly mimics its name sake. For one, the apartment-like dwelling is carved smack-dab in the side of a sandstone cliff like a mythical hideout most kids can only dream of. Second, the spacious living quarters playfully wrap around a central stone pillar, creating an indoor race track of sorts. The property's two porches offer panoramic views of the La Plata River valley. The cave is closed during winter months (December, January, February) and because there is only one unit, booking well in advance is advised. https://www.kokoscave.us/

El Rancho Hotel (Gallup)

The El Rancho Hotel is a New Mexico legend, famous for the many Hollywood stars that stayed there while filming Westerns in the surrounding deserts. Even though its history stretches back for decades, the hotel has been tastefully renovated to include all the modern conveniences discerning travelers demand. https://elranchohotelgallup.com/

Motel Safari (Tucumcari)

Lovingly restored to its historic Route 66 splendor (with modern amenities added, of course), this classic 1950s-style hotel is a trip down memory lane and a fantastic place to find mid-20th-century memorabilia. Murals memorializing the Mother Road adorn its walls and the collection of vintage billboards on the patio is sure to bring a smile or an inquisitive head scratch, depending on the time period in which you were born. Motel Safari is easy to find. Just look for the camel. https://themotelsafari.com/

40. THE NEW MEXICO ART SCENE: TOP 3 PLACES TO EXPERIENCE NEW MEXICAN ART

Santa Fe

Ten years before the pilgrims first set foot on Plymouth Rock, the Spanish established Santa Fe as a permanent colony, making it the second oldest city in the US. The city itself is a work of art, proudly displaying its 'Santa Fe style' that draws on Pueblo Indian and Spanish Territorial architectural traditions.

Thirty-seven years into statehood, New York painter Georgia O'Keeffe relocated to New Mexico, inspired by the state's lighting and landscapes. Her move ignited an Artist Rush with Santa Fe at the center of the wave. Today, the city boasts 250 art galleries and ranks third in the nation for art sales. Don't miss the museum dedicated to this Mother of American Modernism, which is a four-block walk from the Plaza.

Most art galleries in Santa Fe are found along Canyon Road, but what many people don't know is that the State Capitol Building is also an art museum, and it's free! The building contains a number of permanent and temporary exhibits, all fashioned by New Mexican artists.

The Santa Fe Railyard is also a surprisingly great place for art gawking. Dubbed Santa Fe's new gathering place, this kid-friendly, pet-friendly oasis has nearly 20 superb galleries of its own.

Silver City

Despite having only 10,000 residents, festive Silver City enjoys a very vibrant art scene. The town's treasure trove of galleries (50 at last count) features painters, potters, printers, glass blowers, weavers, and jewelry makers. Silver City also has thriving theater and live music communities. This 'event-full' town knows how to party, too, hosting at least a dozen festivals each year, including the Clay Festival, Blues Festival, Chocolate Festival, Written Word Festival, Latin Festival, Print Festival, Hummingbird Festival, and more.

Gallup

A popular stop on Historic Route 66 (it was even mentioned by name in the popular R&B song 'Get

Your Kicks On Route 66' penned by Bobby Troup in 1946), Gallup has served as an important Native American trade center since the late 1800s. Its main streets are lined with culturally-themed murals, historic buildings, trading posts, and curio shops.

The Gallup Arts & Cultural District works closely with Indian artists, helping them showcase and promote their wares. Tourist draws include the monthly Arts Crawl, nightly Native American dances in the summer, a community concert series, and the annual Inter-tribal Indian Ceremonial that features pow-wows, dance shows, art exhibits, rodeos, wine tasting, and more.

41. PARTY LIKE A NEW MEXICAN: THE STATE'S TOP 5 FESTIVALS

New Mexicans know how to party and there are a number of festivals scattered throughout the year that are worth checking out. Below are my Top 5 personal favorites.

International Balloon Fiesta (October in Albuquerque)

Truly one of the man-made wonders of the world, the annual 9-day Albuquerque Balloon Fiesta takes place in early October. Early each morning, more than 500 hot air balloons launch into the crisp blue sky from the city's Balloon Fiesta Park, making it the largest balloon festival in the world. Many people head to Sandia Peak to watch the balloons take off, and rightly so. The top of the peak offers a sweeping view of the Rio Grande Valley. You can, however, see the balloons rise from just about anywhere in the city. http://www.balloonfiesta.com/

Santa Fe Fiesta & Zozobra Burning (September in Santa Fe)

Dating to 1712, Santa Fe's Fiesta is one of the longest running festivals in the country. Complete with mariachi bands, Spanish-style dancing, craft and food booths, parades and more, the celebration officially commemorates Spanish conquistador Don Diego De Vargas' heroic success in recapturing Santa Fe from the Pueblo Indians in 1692.

The unofficial kick-off to the week-long Fiesta celebration is the Zozobra burning. Each September since 1924, a 50-foot Zozobra (i.e., a larger-than-life marionette) is raised on a grand stage in Santa Fe's Fort Marcy Park. Throughout the day, visitors enjoy entertainment by local musicians while writing down their most miserable memories from the past year on small slips of paper. The paper slips are placed in cardboard boxes that are then stuffed inside the Zozobra's long robe. Anticipation builds until late evening when a red-clad Fire Spirit Dancer finally arrives to set alight Old Man Gloom.

Few things are as satisfying (or as cleansing, for that matter) as watching all your misfortune go up in flames, but be advised that hearing the raucous crowd cheer "Burn him, burn him!" in mob-like fashion as the massive Zozobra moans and groans beneath the blaze can be quite unsettling, especially for young children. Viewer discretion advised.
https://www.santafefiesta.org/

Hatch Chile Festival (Labor Day Weekend in Hatch)

As the weather cools, the small town of Hatch heats up with a two-day chile pepper celebration. Hatch is, after all, the Chile Capital of the World.

The festival roughly corresponds with the start of the chile harvest season, which lasts from mid-August through early November. More than 30,000 visitors from all over the world descend on Hatch during Labor Day weekend to sample chile recipes, watch the chile ristra contest, explore artisan stalls and food booths, and enjoy the carnival.

Note that Hatch barely has 2,000 residents and no hotels. You'd best look for accommodation in nearby Truth or Consequences (38 miles north) or Las Cruces (40 miles south).
http://www.hatchchilefest.com/

UFO Festival (July in Roswell)

Each July, more than 20,000 aliens, UFO devotees, and skeptics from all over the world (and universe) descend on the town of Roswell, increasing its population by nearly 50%! The three-day UFO festival immediately follows the country's Fourth of July Celebration—a strategic ploy by city officials to encourage visitors to spend 'just one more day' under Roswell's scorching sun. The celebration of the hotly debated 1947 incident includes a light parade, live entertainment, costume contests (for humans and their pets), guest speakers, and a host of other alien-related activities. http://www.ufofestivalroswell.com/

Totah Festival Indian Market & Pow Wow (Labor Day Weekend in Farmington)

Each Labor Day weekend, the town of Farmington celebrates its Native American heritage with a Cultural Dance Expo, a Navajo rug exhibition & auction, an art contest, and fantastic Native American food (think fry bread and Navajo tacos). Talented Native American artists from across the Southwest set up shop in the Farmington Museum to showcase and sell their wares. The festival has been taking place annually since 1988 and, along with Gallup's Inter-tribal Ceremonial, is one of the best Native American celebrations in New Mexico.
https://www.totahfestival.org/

42. TOP 5 SITES THAT ARE SHROUDED IN MYSTERY

From alien encounters to healing sand to unexplainable works of art, New Mexico is full of mystery and intrigue. Below are five sites guaranteed to make your eyes pop and your jaw drop.

Loretto chapel staircase (Santa Fe)

Back in 1878, the unexpected death of the Loretto chapel's French architect left the Sisters of Loretto with an overwhelming dilemma—how to reach the choir loft without eating up too much of the small chapel's seating area.

To find an answer, the Sisters made a 9-day novena (prayer) to Saint Joseph, the patron saint of carpenters. Shortly thereafter, a mysterious gentleman and his tool-laden burro showed up with a pile of non-native wood and offered to build a set of spiral stairs. He spent the next several months constructing the stairway then disappeared without ever requesting payment, leading the Sisters to surmise he was Joseph of Nazareth himself. But that's only half the miracle. The superbly-built staircase defies the laws of physics since it has no central support column.

Today the sanctuary is a privately-owned wedding chapel that can be visited for a few bucks. An audio recording explains the building's incredible history and architecture in more detail. Be sure to admire the stained-glass windows imported directly from France.

'The Shadow of the Cross' Painting, San Francisco de Asis Church (Rancho de Taos)

Five miles southwest of Taos in the small town of Rancho de Taos stands the most photographed church in all of New Mexico—the Picasso-like San Francisco de Asis adobe church. And we're talking real adobe here, friends, complete with mud, straw and horse hair. While most buildings in Santa Fe and Taos are made to look like adobe using adobe-colored stucco, this church is the real thing. But its authentic adobe architecture isn't the only thing it's famous for. Its minuscule museum houses a mysterious, eyebrow-raising portrait called 'The Shadow of the Cross'.

In the light, the life-size image shows an empty-handed Jesus standing on the Sea of Galilee's shoreline. Turn out the lights, however, and Jesus emerges as a dark, statue-like silhouette carrying a cross on his left shoulder. Some gasp, some faint, some rush out, but all are left wondering, "Just where did that cross come from?" Gives me chills just thinking about it.

Despite years of theories and speculation, this strange and somewhat spooky phenomenon remains an unsolved mystery, even to the barely-known French Canadian artist who painted it.

91

The San Francisco de Asis Church sits to the southeast of New Mexico State Road 68. The museum is located in a small complex on the north side of the church's plaza.

Healing Sand, El Santuario de Chimayo (Chimayo)

According to legend, a group of men were performing penance rituals on Good Friday 1810 when one of them saw a mysterious light protruding from the desert hillside. The man's investigative digging unearthed a simple wooden crucifix, which he delivered to the nearest church in Santa Cruz six miles away.

Before dawn the next morning, the crucifix mysteriously disappeared from the church. It was re-discovered at the site where the man originally found it. Twice more it was brought to the church in Santa Cruz, and twice more it disappeared, only to be found back in its original spot. Many believed the location to be sacred, and while the wooden cross has long since vanished, the legend of the holy dirt where it was found lives on.

Eventually, El Santuario de Chimayo was built atop the site and today draws 300,000 pilgrims a year.

Many believe the dirt possesses restorative healing powers, even though priests admit to refilling the sacred sand pit with soil from outside the church. Regardless, the sanctuary has been nicknamed the 'Lourdes of America' for the many healings that have taken place there. You'll notice a number of crutches hanging on the wall near the pit, left behind by people who no longer needed them after rubbing the magic dirt on their legs. El Santuario is the country's most important Catholic pilgrimage center.

TIP: The sand pit is not located in the chapel itself but sits in a small room just off the main worship area.

Roswell UFO Crash Site (Corona near Roswell)

In July 1947, Roswell suddenly found itself on the map when a local rancher found pieces of unidentifiable debris scattered across his sheep ranch 75 miles outside of town. Suspicions were heightened when the rancher called the Roswell sheriff, who in turn called the Roswell Army-Air Force base. Within hours, soldiers were fanning out across the rancher's field on a government-ordered search-and-rescue mission, whisking away the debris they gathered in heavily armed trucks.

In 1994, nearly 50 years after Roswell's town newspaper first broke the story, the US military finally issued a report linking the incident to a top-secret mission code-named Project Mogul. This highly classified, now declassified, venture resulted in a number of new discoveries, including ultra-lightweight, ultra-strong metals; fiber-optic cables; and fireproof fabrics—the debris of which would have seemed very peculiar to local residents lucky enough to find some back in 1947.

There are still those who support the UFO theory, however, and tens of thousands of believers and skeptics descend on the small town of Roswell and the Corona crash site each year, hoping to learn the truth for themselves—or at least have a little fun in the process.

While three different crash sites claim to be 'the one', only one of them has an official stone marker. That marker is located down a very rough, rattlesnake-laden dirt road where cell phone reception is spotty and GPS service is intermittent at best. Four-wheel-drive vehicles are an absolute must. Be sure you can get in and out in broad daylight to avoid getting lost.

Spoiler alert: In the event you don't make it to the marker, whether by choice or misfortune, the inscription on it reads:

We don't know who they were. We don't know why they came. We only know they changed our view of the universe. This universal sacred site is dedicated July 1997 to the beings who met their destinies near Roswell, New Mexico - July 1947.

While the crash site itself is hard to get to and not recommended, Roswell is worth a stop. Be sure to visit the Alien Zone Café on Roswell's Main Street for a light-hearted alternative to town's text-heavy UFO Museum. For a couple of bucks, you can pose with fake aliens in 20 or so different life-size dioramas—the guaranteed highlight of any trip to the area. http://www.alienzoneroswellnm.com/

The Mission Church at Isleta Pueblo (near Albuquerque)

Back in the mid-18th century, Fray Juan Jose de Padilla was serving as a humble missionary to the Laguna Pueblo people when he was stabbed to death by a number of unidentified assailants. To honor his service and devotion, Padre Padilla (as he was lovingly known) was buried near the altar of the Isleta

Pueblo's 17th-century church. Over the next 63 years, his un-embalmed body mysteriously rose to the surface a number of times—his clothes, skin, and hair perfectly intact as the day he died.

The dry New Mexican climate undoubtedly played a role in his preservation, but could not explain why more than 60 years after his death his body was still supple, moist, and fragrant. Roman Catholic authorities deemed the esteemed friar 'incorruptible'—an honor granted to saintly individuals whose corpses unexplainably escape the ravages of time. The church has been a pilgrimage site ever since.

In 1960, the church finally paved over what had been a dirt then wooden floor for centuries. Neither a shake nor a knock from Padre Padilla has been heard ever since, leaving parishioners to wonder if he is finally at rest or frantically banging on the cement floor that now muffles his sounds and prevents his escape.

The church is part of the Isleta Pueblo and is located 19 miles south of Albuquerque near the town of Bosque Farms.

43. TOP 5 OTHERWORLDLY LANDSCAPES

New Mexican deserts are literally and figuratively 'the bomb'. Yes, the state's Chihuahuan Desert is so desolate and remote that Manhattan Project scientists decided to explode the world's first atomic bomb there, but not all of our deserts are worthy of destruction.

Most of our desert landscapes contain spectacular scenery that quite simply cannot be found anywhere else. Below are my Top 5 favorite spots.

Tent Rocks National Monument (near Santa Fe)

Kasha-Katuwe or 'tent rocks' in English was only designated a national monument in 2001. The monument's valley is filled with white-striped rock formations that widen at the bottom and narrow at the top, resembling teepees (hence the name 'tent rocks'). Despite its national status, the Cochiti Pueblo Tribal Governor officially controls the land and has been known to close the park at will. Follow the marked trail to the observation point for a sweeping view of the area.

To get to Tent Rocks from Santa Fe, head south on I-25 to NM Highway 16 (Exit 264—Cochiti Pueblo). Turn right onto NM Highway 22 and follow the signs. Note that the area is prone to flash flooding so be sure to head any warnings.

Ah-Shi-Sle-Pah Wilderness Study Area (near Bloomfield)

A wonderland of weathered rocks, Ah-Shi-Sle-Pah's mounds are as mysterious as the area's name. The valley boasts an impressive array of pyramid-shaped, mushroom-shaped, and chimney-shaped hoodoos (tall, thin rock spires jutting up from a basin or badland, for those of you who don't know what hoodoos are) as well as an abundance of plant and animal fossils.

I won't lie by telling you this place is easy to get to. Ah-Shi-Sle-Pah is even more remote than the nearby Bisti Badlands and much more difficult to access. Take US Highway 550 south from Bloomfield to NM 57 then be prepared for a bumpy ride down 15 miles of unsealed road once the paving ends. A high-clearance vehicle is recommended for the last half mile, but you can always walk if you don't happen to have one.

The most dramatic formations are within one to two miles of the parking area. The walking path is flat, which means the highlights can easily be seen in half a day. Expect to see no one and come prepared with plenty of water, sunscreen, and a good GPS for finding your way back to your car.

Bisti Badlands (near Farmington)

Had aliens landed here instead of Roswell in 1947, they just might have stuck around. This soul-stirring landscape is otherworldly enough to satisfy even the most discriminating alien life forms, and human encounters here are few and far between.

Created by millennia of slow-moving water, these odd-looking spectacles of Mother Nature abound at every turn (once you arrive, that is—the formations are a good mile-and-a-half by foot from the parking area). Petrified tortoise shells on a stick, perhaps? Or maybe fossilized giant mushrooms? Children and adults alike will have fun finding shapes in these implausible, top-heavy lumps of clay, just as much as they enjoy finding shapes in passing clouds.

The best access point is found on Road 7297 off NM State Highway 371 about 40 miles south of Farmington. Road 7297 is gravel and can be prone to flash flooding. You'll hit a T-junction about two miles down. Turn left and drive another mile to the Bisti Access Parking Area. Note that there is neither water nor toilets (not even a port-a-potty) at the parking lot and no official signage to lead you to the rock formations. Don't let this deter or detour you, however. Simply proceed with caution or go with a local who knows the area well.

Ship Rock (Shiprock)

Looking like, well…a ship…sailing across a vast sea of nothingness, this ancient volcanic plug is believed by Navajos to have been a giant bird that brought their ancestors to the area before promptly turning to stone. My dad used to tell me how my grandparents climbed Ship Rock for their honeymoon—a daunting task by today's standards, let alone those of the late 1930s.

The rock is only accessible by four-wheel drive vehicles and climbing it today is illegal (sort of). It's best viewed from a distance anyway (IMHO). You really can't miss it when traveling on US Highway 64 between Shiprock and the New Mexico-Arizona state line.

White Sands National Monument (near Alamogordo)

Where else in the good ol' U. S. of A. can you walk barefoot among mounds of sparkling, flour-like gypsum crystals pulverized by millennia of wind and rain? Nowhere. Moving at a rate of 30 feet per year, this active dune field is a favorite with hikers, photographers, and sledders. Yes, you read that right. Sledders. Bring your own or buy one at the Visitors Center to go cruising down the dunes at break-neck speed (ok, maybe not that fast, but still a good ride nonetheless).

The Visitors Center is located on US Highway 70 less than 20 miles southwest of Alamogordo.

44. TOP 5 'OTHER' OUTDOOR PLACES TO EXPLORE

Whitewater Canyon Catwalk, Gila National Forest (near Glenwood)

Whitewater Canyon has been a favorite hiding place for outlaws and Indians since the 19th century. Geronimo and his band of Apache warriors hid from the US Army here. So did Butch Cassidy and his gang when they tried to ditch the Pinkerton detectives who were hot on their trail. Nowadays visitors consist mostly of locals and tourists looking to hide from the heat of the sun and dodge not detectives or military personnel but the stresses of modern-day living. The catwalk is located five miles northeast of Glenwood.

Cumbres & Toltec Railway (Chama)

The Cumbres & Toltec Railway reaches a staggering height of 10,015 feet, making it the highest rail route in the United States. Originally built to serve silver miners in New Mexico & Colorado during the 1880s, this historic train route passes through some of the state's most spectacular mountain scenery. A highlight for many is Tanglefoot Curve, a loop so tight the engine almost rejoins the caboose.

Trains leave daily from Chama, New Mexico and Antonito, Colorado and cross the New Mexico-Colorado state line a whopping 11 times. Regardless of where you depart from, the train will stop in Osier, Colorado for a lunch buffet that's included in the ticket price. https://cumbrestoltec.com/

Cosmic Campground (near Glenwood)

The obscure Cosmic Campground is the first designated International Dark-Sky Sanctuary in North America and one of only four in the world. What is an 'International Dark-Sky Sanctuary', you ask? Well, by the International Dark-Sky Association's definition, it's a piece of land possessing an exceptional or distinguished quality of starry nights. The barren campground is, after all, 40 miles from the nearest 'major' artificial light source and 13 miles north of tiny Glenwood on Highway 180 (Glenwood has a population of less than 150, by the way).

To get here, travel south on US Highway 180 from Glenwood, turn west on Ranger Station Road, and watch for the signs. If you reach Smokey Drive, you've gone too far. Come here on a clear night and prepare to be gob-smacked.

And as a bonus while you're in the neighborhood, be sure to visit Gila National Forest—the first spot to ever become a protected US Wilderness Area. The place is a bird watchers paradise with bald eagles, golden eagles, blue herons, black hawks, and migratory birds like cranes, geese and ducks often sited.

Rio Grande Gorge (near Taos)

Traveling west on US Highway 64 toward Taos, you'll be required to pass over the second highest bridge in the US Highway System (the highest is at Royal Gorge, Colorado, for all you lovers of useless trivia out there). Pullouts near the bridge allow you to leave your car and walk across. The drop to the Rio Grande River below is significant and the view is quite literally breathtaking. I remember crossing the bridge once with my fidgety 11-month-old daughter in arms. Talk about nerve-racking. I don't believe I've ever held on to her (or anything) so tightly.

Santa Rosa Blue Hole (Santa Rosa)

Move over, Belize. New Mexico's got a famous blue hole, too! The crystal-clear water of the Santa Rosa Blue Hole camouflages a network of underwater caves that were virtually unexplored until 2013. Located just off historic Route 66 and I-40, the 80-feet-deep natural pool was a popular swimming oasis for road-tripping families traversing an otherwise monotonous desert. Swimming remains free-of-charge, just as it was in the Mother Road's prime. The water is a cool 62°F (16.7°C) year-round. https://www.santarosabluehole.com

45. TOP 5 KITSCHY CURIOSITIES WORTH A PHOTO (OR A LISTEN)

Giant Chile Pepper (Las Cruces)

It only seems right that the state famous for its chile peppers would boast the largest one in the world. The 47-feet-long, 5,000-pound red hot chile pepper was built primarily to attract visitors to the adjacent two-star Big Chile Inn…and to put Las Cruces on the map, or so the story goes. According to many, Las Cruces has tried numerous tactics to wrestle away from Hatch the 'Chile Capital of the World' title. Walk right up to the statue any time of day and be sure to visit the hotel's free chile pepper gardens for a close-up look at the crop. You'll find both in the heart of Las Cruces on US Highway 70, also known as Picacho Road.

Giant Pistachio (Alamogordo)

Kitschy roadside eyesores don't get much nuttier than the 30-feet-tall giant pistachio towering over Alamogordo. Surprisingly real-looking, the shell-encased nut is part 'photo op', part 'advertisement' for the gift shop at Tom McGinn's PistachioLand

105

Ranch and Winery, lovingly labeled the nuttiest place in New Mexico. The shop is definitely worth a peek, especially for its wide range of pistachio products and free pistachio tasting bar. And heck, if you're really into pistachios, why not take home a tree? Grafted pistachio trees are available for sale each February.

PistachioLand is located seven miles north of Alamogordo on the stretch of road where US Highways 54 and 70 merge.

Tumbleweed Snowman (Albuquerque)

Detached from their roots and tossed to and fro by the wind, tumbleweeds are a common site along New Mexico's roadways. Lamenting the city's lack of snow in 1995, the Albuquerque Metropolitan Arroyo Flood Control Authority (AMAFCA) decided to recycle the near-useless dead plants by fashioning them into a 14-foot jolly snowman. The snowman has since become the unofficial mascot of Albuquerque's holiday season and proudly stands in the same spot near AMAFCA's offices (visible from I-40) each year from late November to early January.

Recycled Roadrunner (near Las Cruces)

Rising above I-10 just ten miles west of Las Cruces, this two-story roadrunner was built solely from scrap metal and other waste products. Aimed at inspiring onlookers to consider the impact of consumption and waste, it's gone through a few upgrades in recent years but continues to shine soulfully in the New Mexico sun. Please note there is a scenic pullout for those who would like to take pictures. Using the pullout is much safer than pulling over to the side of the road as this stretch of I-10 tends to be quite busy.

Musical Highway (Tijeras near Albuquerque)

Back in 2014, the Tijeras division of the New Mexico Department of Transportation came up with a brilliant idea to get locals and visitors alike to slow down on a sleepy stretch of old Route 66 just outside the city. They added rumble strips to a quarter-mile section of the road that were engineered and properly spaced to sound like the patriotic song, "America The Beautiful". But there's a catch! Drivers must be going exactly 45 miles per hour (the posted speed limit) in order for the rumble strips to work. The aptly named 'Musical Highway' is located on eastbound Route

333 (part of old Route 66) between mile markers 4 and 5.

46. TOP 5 PLACES TO EXPERIENCE THE WILD WEST

Few states embody the lawless, rough-and-tumble American frontier better than New Mexico. The state's geography, monuments, legends and folklore speak loud and proud about this important chapter in US history. Those seeking to experience a bit of the Wild West will find no shortage of venues in New Mexico. Below are my Top 5 recommended favorites.

El Rancho de las Golondrinas (Santa Fe)

An historic 18th-century ranch turned living history museum, El Rancho was once an important 'paraje' (or 'rest stop') on the famous Camino Real that led from Mexico City to Santa Fe in the days of Spanish occupation.

Please note that El Rancho is quite large (meaning it takes time to walk all 200-acres) and lies at over 7,000 feet in elevation (take it easy and breathe deep). With loads of hands-on activities, you may want to avoid visiting the ranch during October's Spanish Colonial Days when thousands of school children

from around the state descend on the property.
https://www.golondrinas.org/

Farm & Ranch Heritage Museum (Las Cruces)

Ranked by TripAdvisor as the #1 attraction in Las Cruces, this interactive, living history museum brings to life New Mexico's rural heritage by highlighting 4,000 years of farming and ranching traditions. Yes, you read that right. 4,000 years! Pioneer skills like blacksmithing, dowsing, weaving, and quilting are showcased regularly on weekends. Since most of the museum's attractions are outdoors, visitors should plan for sun in the summer and cold in the winter. http://www.nmfarmandranchmuseum.org/

Kit Carson House (Taos)

Christopher 'Kit' Carson is one of American's most folkloric frontiersmen. Kit ran away to New Mexico at the young age of 16 by way of the newly opened Santa Fe Trail that flowed past his Missouri home. Using Taos as his base, the brave young lad went on to become a fur trapper, mountain man, wilderness guide, scout, Indian agent, courier, and eventually an officer in the US Army.

In 1843, Kit laid down permanent roots in Taos by purchasing a territorial-style adobe house near the town's main Plaza. He and his third wife lived there for 25 years, raising eight children (seven of which were born in the home) and fostering several Indian youths. The Kit Carson House offers a poignant and very personal glimpse into the life of one of America's most idolized Western heroes. http://www.kitcarsonmuseum.org/

Lincoln Historic Site (Lincoln)

This time-capsule-of-a-town is by far New Mexico's most visited historical attraction and looks like a real-life movie set for old-time Westerns. Appearing much as it did in 1880, Lincoln showcases 17 historic buildings, including a mercantile mart stocked with real 19th-century goods in original cases and shelving.

Lincoln was made famous (or infamous, depending on your perspective) during the four-year Lincoln County War—quite possibly the bloodiest confrontation in the history of the Wild West and one that prompted US President Rutherford B. Hayes to label the one-street town 'the Most Dangerous Street in America'.

Outlaw and federal fugitive, Billy the Kid, loaned his gun-slinging hand to the skirmish, murdering three people before it was all said and done (two of which were the deputies guarding his cell). His break from the Lincoln County jail was the most celebrated of his short 21-year life and is commemorated each August in a local pageant.
http://www.nmhistoricsites.org/lincoln/

Palace of the Governors (Santa Fe)

Few buildings have experienced the kind of history that Santa Fe's Palace of the Governors has. If only walls could talk.

This historic edifice served as the seat of government for Spain's Nuevo Mexico colony for nearly 200 years and became New Mexico's first territorial capital following the United States' victory in the Mexican-American War.

Between 1909 and 2009, the building served as the Museum of New Mexico. It has since been revamped and rededicated to replicate and retell its extensive 400-year history as the country's oldest public building still in use. You'll find it on the north side of downtown Santa Fe's historic Plaza.
http://www.palaceofthegovernors.org/

47. TOP 5 MUST-SEE HISTORICAL MARKERS

Santa Fe Trail Marker (Santa Fe)

Santa Fe's historic Plaza in the heart of downtown marks the terminus for both the Spanish El Camino Real de Tierra Adentro (The Royal Road of the Interior Land) and the Mexican & American Santa Fe Trail.

The 1,600-mile Camino Real operated between Mexico City and Santa Fe between 1598 and 1882, bringing settlers, goods, and information to Santa Fe and crops, livestock, and crafts to the markets of greater Mexico.

Following Mexican independence in 1821, the country was opened to foreign trade. The Santa Fe Trail, which operated between the Mexican city of Santa Fe and the American city of St. Louis, Missouri, provided an essential link between the two economies for more than 60 years.

The marker stands at the southeast corner of Santa Fe's Plaza. If you're lucky, you just might find a cart selling fresh tamales nearby. The cart tends to be out during the height of the tourist season.

Trinity Site Marker (near San Antonio & Socorro)

'Trinity' was the code name for the detonation of the world's first atomic bomb. Trinity Site is the place where the experimental weapon was first exploded. US military officials may not have understood the long-term impact (pun intended) plutonium devices would have on human life, but Trinity gave them a good indication of what would happen on initial contact. The atomic fireball obliterated trees, morphed sand into glass (which is what happens when sand gets really, really hot), and shattered windows as far away as 120 miles.

Trinity remains a military site and is only open to the public on the first Saturdays of April and October. Come prepared to show proper ID and be willing to follow instructions. If you can't make it in April or October, a contemplative historic marker can be found near the Stallion Gate turnoff for the site on US Highway 380.

Trinity Site is situated 40 miles southeast of San Antonio on US Highway 380. Socorro, the largest town in the area, is 10 miles north of San Antonio.

Bataan Death March Statue (Las Cruces)

The jungle-laden Bataan peninsula on the Philippine island of Luzon is best known for the Allied troops' failed fight against Japanese invaders in March of 1942. Following their surrender, 78,000 Americans and Filipinos were forced by their captors to march to prison camps 65 miles away. Nearly 15% lost their lives to illness, thirst, or execution before they arrived.

The now-infamous Bataan Death March is memorialized by a series of federally funded bronze statues in Las Cruces' Veterans Park—the first of their kind. Why Las Cruces, you ask? Because a greater percentage of New Mexicans served as prisoners of war to the Japanese than of any other US state.

Veterans Park is located on Roadrunner Parkway in Las Cruces, which runs parallel to I-25.

Bosque Redondo Memorial (near Fort Sumner and Santa Rosa)

This monument honors the years of persecution that the Navajo and Mescalero Apache suffered at the hands of the US Army. In what became known as The Long Walk of 1864, as many as 10,000 Navajos were marched 300 miles from their homeland in northwestern New Mexico to be incarcerated at the Bosque Redondo Reservation, where the memorial now stands.

The deportation and attempted ethnic cleansing of the Navajo continued for several years before the ill-conceived reservation was finally closed in 1868. Nearly a third of those forcibly removed to the reservation died. Those who survived were eventually returned to their homes. Several Apache tribesmen were also held at the Bosque Redondo fort.

The monument is located in Fort Sumner 51 miles south of Santa Rosa on US Highway 84. To get to the monument from Fort Sumner, take US Highway 60/84 three miles east to Billy the Kid Road. The plaque is then three and a half miles south.

Four Corners National Monument (near Shiprock)

Four Corners, as it's called locally, is the only quadripoint of its kind in the United States, and this rare geographic oddity attracts over a quarter-million visitors each year. During peak season (summer), camera-clicking tourists line up to strike a pose on the little bronze circle that proves they were in all four

115

states at the same time (or does it?). Admission is charged per person, not per vehicle, and because the site is operated by the Navajo & Ute tribal governments, National Park and State Park passes are not valid.

To get there from Shiprock, travel west on US Highway 64 to Teec Nos Pos, Arizona, turn north on to US Highway 160, then make a final turn onto Tribal Road 597.

48. FOUR CORNERS IS OFF-MARK (BUT SO WHAT?)

The Four Corners quadripoint is one of many by-products of America's Civil War. Back in the early 1860s, some residents of the enormous New Mexico Territory wanted to join the Confederacy and tried to become their own territory to do so. Thus, Arizona was born of New Mexico.

Confederate maps show the two horizontal territories of New Mexico and Arizona stacked one on top of the other. In 1863, the Union decided to separate them, not north and south but east and west by continuing the Utah-Colorado territorial line down to the border with Mexico. Survey equipment at the time was of course rudimentary by today's standards and, to make a long story short, the Four Corners Monument is off by exactly 1,807.14 feet from where it was originally intended to be, according to the National Geodetic Survey.

Wandering borders weren't unusual back in the day, though this particular boundary dispute was escalated all the way to the United States Supreme Court, which ruled in 1925 that the initial survey would remain 'official'. That should have put things to rest, but every so often students from nearby San Juan College and other institutes of higher learning resurvey the border and make a ruckus about the line's incorrect position. That all matters very little, of course, if you're trying to get your picture taken while standing on the four-state marker or buying Native American food or souvenirs, all of which are only available at the current monument.

49. TAKE YOUR PIC: NEW MEXICO'S 5 MOST PHOTOGENIC TOWNS

While New Mexico has more than its fair share of picture-perfect towns, these five are my most photo-worthy favorites.

Chimayo

Listed as one of Budget Travel's Most Beautiful Towns in the World, mystical Chimayo is famous for its hand-woven tapestries and the healing power of its santuario's sand (refer back to section 42 for more details). The peaceful town was founded by Spanish settlers in the late 17th century and is nestled at the base of New Mexico's Sangre de Cristo mountain range—a splendid backdrop for the town's adobe architecture.

Las Vegas

This cultural hot spot makes the list because 900 of its buildings are featured on the National Register of Historic Places. The town is an architectural treasure chest, showcasing Victorian buildings from its railroading past and mission-style structures from its humble beginnings as a Mexican land grant. Don't miss Plaza Park in the heart of the city, which is considered the prettiest plaza in the American Southwest.

Ruidoso

In Spanish, Ruidoso means noisy, but only recently has this quaint mountain town begun living up to its name. Once secluded and barely known outside the state, Ruidoso is now booming. Named for the rushing Rio Ruidoso (noisy river) that runs through the center of town, outdoor enthusiasts flock here to enjoy the countless hiking, biking and rafting opportunities the community and its surroundings have to offer. The town's quaint shops and eye-popping scenery will satisfy everyone else.

Silver City

Another city with an enviable accolade—one of Budget Travel's Top 10 Coolest American Small Towns—Silver City was, as its name suggests, an 1870s silver mining town. Its colorful past includes the dubious honor of being the first town to arrest famous New Mexican outlaw, Billy the Kid. Today its flourishing art scene, up-and-coming food scene, and historic downtown make pinon-spackled Silver City a great place to spend a day and take a picture.

Taos

Dubbed one of the World's Prettiest Mountain Towns by Travel and Leisure magazine, artsy Taos is famous for its scenic location, historic architecture, and its art. Entranced by its seemingly effortless

119

beauty, photographers like Ansel Adams and painters like Georgia O'Keeffe have been coming to Taos since the early 20th century. The still-inhabited Taos Pueblo just outside of town is said to be the most photographed structure in all of New Mexico, and the area's four ski resorts in the nearby Sangre de Cristo mountain range make Taos a year-round destination.

50. AMERICA'S SUNSET CAPITAL: TOP 5 PLACES TO WATCH THE SUN GO DOWN

Did you know that New Mexico is the undisputed Sunset Capital of the World? Ok, so maybe 'undisputed' is a bit of a stretch, but New Mexico's desert landscapes and dry air do produce some pretty incredible sunsets. While there isn't really a bad place to watch the sun go down in New Mexico, here are my Top 5 favorite locations:

Bisti Badlands (near Farmington)

Bisti is one of those special places that makes you feel like you've left one planet for another. Mushroom-shaped mounds cast shadows at every turn while the vibrant colors of the surrounding strata seem to deepen as the sun descends. The place is difficult to find and, with no clearly marked trails, you will need to make certain you can find your way back once the light has left.

If Bisti sunsets intimidate you, the bluffs surrounding the nearby town of Farmington offer sweeping sunset views clear out to Ship Rock (30 miles away) and Angel Peak (also 30 miles away). FYI, the terms 'bluff', 'butte', and 'plateau' are used interchangeably in this part of the country, though 'bluff' is by far the most common.

Refer to Section 43 for driving directions to Bisti.

Carlsbad Caverns (near Carlsbad)

While sunsets may not be as stunning from the mouth of the caverns as they are from the other viewpoints mentioned here, it is simply spectacular to watch a black cloud of bats emerge from the cave each evening, framed by a dusky-purple sky. Even better is the fact that because Carlsbad Caverns is a National Park (New Mexico's only), concrete stadium seating is available from which spectators can enjoy the event.

Carlsbad Caverns National Park is located at the end of the scenic seven-mile Carlsbad Caverns Highway—the park's only access road. You'll find the Highway about 20 miles southwest of the town of Carlsbad.

Ghost Ranch (Abiquiu near Espanola)

One look at the rusty orange- and yellow-striped hills of Ghost Ranch and you'll understand why New York artist Georgia O'Keeffe set up shop here. Ghost Ranch vistas and fauna were the subject of many of her most iconic paintings. Come early and visit this Mother of American Modernism's art studio, then stick around to watch the sun go down.

Ghost Ranch is located 14 miles northwest of Abiquiu on US Highway 84.

Sandia Peak (Albuquerque)

The observation deck atop Albuquerque's 10,378-foot Sandia Peak offers an unobstructed view of the 11,000 square-mile Rio Grande River Valley below. With little to obstruct this 'view from on high' and a fairly flat horizon in the distance, the sun takes longer to set here than almost anywhere else in the state. Don't miss it!

For the tram's hours of operation, visit http://www.sandiapeak.com. You can also drive to the top of Sandia Peak.

White Sands National Monument (near Las Cruces)

What can be better than watching brilliant hues of orange, red, yellow, and purple spread across the sky over gypsum-covered hills? There are no words.

See Section 43 for location details.

BONUS SPOT: Very Large Array (Socorro)

Western New Mexico's scrub brush-laden landscape may seem 'good-for-nothing' but it's an ideal location for the Very Large Array (VLA), a 100-square-mile stretch of massive white radio telescopes that scan the skies for alien life forms, black holes, supernovae, quasars, pulsars, astrophysical masers, and other cool space 'events'.

The VLA gladly welcomes guests from 8:30 AM to dusk year-round. A stroll through the dishes at sunset is especially surreal, as the dishes cast long shadows across the flat desert plain.

The VLA is situated 50 miles west of Socorro. From US Highway 60, turn south onto New Mexico Highway 52 then west onto the VLA access road. Signs will guide you from there.

TOP REASONS TO BOOK THIS TRIP

Our Food: New Mexico is known for its flavorful food and boasts its own signature cuisine. This tasty blend of Native American, Spanish, and Mexican cooking styles has been adapted and refined over 400 years. Simply put, there are smells, tastes, and menu items in New Mexico you won't find anywhere else.

Our History: Whether you're seeking Native American culture, Spanish colony history, a taste of the Wild West, Route 66 memorabilia, or modern stories of scientific discoveries and aliens, New Mexico's history offers something for everyone.

Our Landscapes: With pine tree-covered mountains and juniper-covered hills, bubbling hot springs and foreboding deserts, crystal-white gypsum sand dunes and dusty-dry grasslands, intergalactic landscapes and ancient volcanic cones, New Mexico has much to offer when it comes to geographic diversity.

Our People: New Mexico is a state loaded with ethnic variety. Twenty-three Native American tribes, the country's largest per-capita Hispanic population, a number of Wild West cowboy clusters, and more artists per capita than any other state all call New Mexico home. New Mexicans are diverse, friendly, down-to-earth, and welcoming.

Our Skies: New Mexico's high altitude, thin air, dry climate, and minimal artificial light pollution make for some pretty amazing sunrises, sunsets, and star-gazing.

Our Solitude: Size-wise, New Mexico is the country's fifth largest state. Population-wise, it ranks 45th. That means you'll almost have the place to yourself. Even our largest cities are comparatively small and free of the hustle and bustle so typical of America's megapolises.

BONUS BOOK

50 THINGS TO KNOW ABOUT PACKING LIGHT FOR TRAVEL

PACK THE RIGHT WAY EVERY TIME

AUTHOR: MANIDIPA BHATTACHARYYA

Disclaimer: The publisher has put forth an effort in preparing and arranging this book. The information provided herein by the author is provided "as is". Use this information at your own risk. The publisher is not a licensed doctor. Consult your doctor before engaging in any medical activities. The publisher and author disclaim any liabilities for any loss of profit or commercial or personal damages resulting from the information contained in this book.

Edited by Melanie Howthorne

ABOUT THE AUTHOR

Manidipa Bhattacharyya is a creative writer and editor, with an education in English literature and Linguistics. After working in the IT industry for seven long years she decided to call it quits and follow her heart instead. Manidipa has been ghost writing, editing, proof reading and doing secondary research services for many story tellers and article writers for about three years. She stays in Kolkata, India with her husband and a busy two year old. In her own time Manidipa enjoys travelling, photography and writing flash fiction.

Manidipa believes in travelling light and never carries anything that she couldn't haul herself on a trip. However, travelling with her child changed the scenario. She seemed to carry the entire world with her for the baby on the first two trips. But good sense prevailed and she is again working her way to becoming a light traveler, this time with a kid.

INTRODUCTION

He who would travel happily
must travel light.

-Antoine de Saint-Exupéry

Travel takes you to different places from seas and mountains to deserts and much more. In your travels you get to interact with different people and their cultures. You will, however, enjoy the sights and interact positively with these new people even more, if you are travelling light.

When you travel light your mind can be free from worry about your belongings. You do not have to spend precious vacation time waiting for your luggage to arrive after a long flight. There is be no chance of your bags going missing and the best part is that you need not pay a fee for checked baggage.

People who have mastered this art of packing light will root for you to take only one carry-on, wherever you go. However, many people can find it really hard to pack light. More so if you are travelling with children. Differentiating between "must have" and "just in case" items is the starting point. There will be ample shopping avenues at your destination which are just waiting to be explored.

This book will show you 'packing' in a new 'light' – pun intended – and help you to embrace light packing practices for all of your future travels.

Off to packing!

DEDICATION

I dedicate this book to all the travel buffs that I know, who have given me great insights into the contents of their backpacks.

THE RIGHT TRAVEL GEAR

1. CHOOSE YOUR TRAVEL GEAR CAREFULLY

While selecting your travel gear, pick items that are light weight, durable and most importantly, easy to carry. There are cases with wheels so you can drag them along – these are usually on the heavy side because of the trolley. Alternatively a backpack that you can carry comfortably on your back, or even a duffel bag that you can carry easily by hand or sling across your body are also great options. Whatever you choose, one thing to keep in mind is that the luggage itself should not weigh a ton, this will give you the flexibility to bring along one extra pair of shoes if you so desire.

2. CARRY THE MINIMUM NUMBER OF BAGS

Selecting light weight luggage is not everything. You need to restrict the number of bags you carry as well. One carry-on size bag is ideal for light travel. Most carriers allow one cabin baggage plus one purse, handbag or camera bag as long as it slides under the seat in front. So technically, you can carry two items of luggage without checking them in.

3. PACK ONE EXTRA BAG

Always pack one extra empty bag along with your essential items. This could be a very light weight duffel bag or even a sturdy tote bag which takes up minimal space. In the event that you end up buying a lot of souvenirs, you already have a handy bag to stuff all that into and do not have to spend time hunting for an appropriate bag.

I'm very strict with my packing and have everything in its right place. I never change a rule. I hardly use anything in the hotel room. I wheel my own wardrobe in and that's it.

Charlie Watts

CLOTHES & ACCESSORIES

4. PLAN AHEAD

Figure out in advance what you plan to do on your trip. That will help you to pick that one dress you need for the occasion. If you are going to attend a wedding then you have to carry formal wear. If not, you can ditch the gown for something lighter that will be comfortable during long walks or on the beach.

5. WEAR THAT JACKET

Remember that wearing items will not add extra luggage for your air travel. So wear that bulky jacket that you plan to carry for your trip. This saves space and can also help keep you warm during the chilly flight.

6. MIX AND MATCH

Carry clothes that can be interchangeably used to reinvent your look. Find one top that goes well with a couple of pairs of pants or skirts. Use tops, shirts and jackets wisely along with other accessories like a scarf or a stole to create a new look.

7. CHOOSE YOUR FABRIC WISELY

Stuffing clothes in cramped bags definitely takes its toll which results in wrinkles. It is best to carry wrinkle free, synthetic clothes or merino tops. This will eliminate the need for that small iron you usually bring along.

8. DITCH CLOTHES PACK UNDERWEAR

Pack more underwear and socks. These are the things that will give you a fresh feel even if you do not get a chance to wear fresh clothes. Moreover these are easy to wash and can be dried inside the hotel room itself.

9. CHOOSE DARK OVER LIGHT

While picking your clothes choose dark coloured ones. They are easy to colour coordinate and can last longer before needing a wash. Accidental food spills and dirt from the road are less visible on darker clothes.

10. WEAR YOUR JEANS

Take only one pair of Jeans with you, which you should wear on the flight. Remember to pick a pair that can be worn for sightseeing trips and is equally eloquent for dinner. You can add variety by adding light weight cargoes and chinos.

11. CARRY SMART ACCESSORIES

The right accessory can give you a fresh look even with the same old dress. An intelligent neck-piece, a couple of bright scarves, stoles or a sarong can be used in a number of ways to add variety to your clothing. These light weight beauties can double up as a nursing cover, a light blanket, beach wear, a modesty cover for visiting places of worship, and also makes for an enthralling game of peek-a-boo.

12. LEARN TO FOLD YOUR GARMENTS

Seasoned travellers all swear by rolling their clothes for compact and wrinkle free packing. Bundle packing, where you roll the clothes around a central object as if tying it up, is also a popular method of compact and wrinkle free packing. Stacking folded clothes one on top of another is a big no-no as it makes creases extreme and they are difficult to get rid of without ironing.

13. WASH YOUR DIRTY LAUNDRY

One of the ways to avoid carrying loads of clothes is to wash the clothes you carry. At some places you might get to use the laundry services or a Laundromat but if you are in a pinch, best solution is to wash them yourself. If that is the plan then carrying quick drying clothes is highly recommended, which most often also happen to be the wrinkle free variety.

14. LEAVE THOSE TOWELS BEHIND

Regular towels take up a lot of space, are heavy and take ages to dry out. If you are staying at hotels they will provide you with towels anyway. If you are travelling to a remote place, where the availability of towels look doubtful, carry a light weight travel towel of viscose material to do the job.

15. USE A COMPRESSION BAG

Compression bags are getting lots of recommendation now days from regular travellers. These are useful for saving space in your luggage when you have to pack bulky dresses. While packing for the return trip, get help from the hotel staff to arrange a vacuum cleaner.

FOOTWEAR

16. PUT ON YOUR HIKING BOOTS

If you have plans to go hiking or trekking during your trip, you will need those bulky hiking boots. The best way to carry them is to wear them on flight to save space and luggage weight. You can remove the boots once inside and be comfortable in your socks.

17. PICKING THE RIGHT SHOES

Shoes are often the bulkiest items, along with being the dainty if you are a female. They need care and take up a lot of space in your luggage. It is advisable therefore to pick shoes very carefully. If you plan to do a lot of walking and site seeing, then wearing a pair of comfortable walking shoes are a must. For more formal occasions you can carry durable, light weight flats which will not take up much space.

18. STUFF SHOES

If you happen to pack a pair of shoes, ensure you utilize their hollow insides. Tuck small items like rolled up socks or belts to save space. They will also be easy to find.

TOILETRIES

19. STASHING TOILETRIES

Carry only absolute necessities. Airline rules dictate that for one carry-on bag, liquids and gels must be in 3.4 ounce (100ml) bottles or less, and must be packed in a one quart zip-lock bag. If you are planning to stay in a hotel, the basic things will be provided for you. It's best is to buy the rest from the local market at your destination.

20. TAKE ALONG TAMPONS

Tampons are a hard to find item in a lot of countries. Figure out how many you need and pack accordingly. For longer stays you can buy them online and have them delivered to where you are staying.

21. GET PAMPERED BEFORE YOU TRAVEL

Some avid travellers suggest getting a pedicure and manicure just the day before travelling. This not only gives you a well kept look, you also save the trouble of packing nail polish. Remember, every little bit of weight reduced adds up.

ELECTRONICS

22. LUGGING ALONG ELECTRONICS

Electronics have a large role to play in our lives today. Most of us cannot imagine our lives away from our phones, laptops or tablets. However while travelling, one must consider the amount of weight these electronics add to our luggage. Thankfully smart phones come along with all the essentials tools like a camera, email access, picture editing tools and more. They are smart to the point of eliminating the need to carry multiple gadgets. Choose a smart phone that suits all your requirements and travel with the world in your palms or pocket.

23. REDUCE THE NUMBER OF CHARGERS

If you do travel with multiple electronic devices, you will have to bear the additional burden of carrying all their chargers too. Check if a single charger can be used for multiple devices. You might also consider investing in a pocket charger. These small devices support multiple devices while keeping you charged on the go.

24. TRAVEL FRIENDLY APPS

Along with smart phones come numerous apps, which are immensely helpful in our travels. You name it and you have an app for it at hand – take pictures, sharing with friends and family, torch to light dark roads, maps, checking flight/train times, find hotels and many other things. Use these smart alternatives to traditional items like books to eliminate weight and save space.

> *I get ideas about what's essential*
> *when packing my suitcase.*

-Diane von Furstenberg

TRAVELLING WITH KIDS

25. BRING ALONG THE STROLLER

Kids might enjoy walking for a while but they soon tire out and a stroller is the just the right thing for them to rest in while you continue your tour. Strollers also double duty as a luggage carrier and shopping bag holder. Remember to pick a light weight, easy to handle brand of stroller. Better yet, find out in advance if you can rent a stroller at your destination.

26. BRING ONLY ENOUGH DIAPERS FOR YOUR TRIP

Diapers take up a lot of space and add to the weight of your luggage. Therefore it is advisable to carry just enough diapers to last through the trip and a few for afterwards, till you buy fresh stock at your destination. Unless of course you are travelling to a really remote area, in which case you have no choice but to carry the load. Otherwise diapers are something you will find pretty easily.

27. TAKE ONLY A COUPLE OF TOYS

Children are easily attracted by new things in their environment. While travelling they will find numerous 'new' objects to scrutinize and play with. Packing just one favorite toy is enough, or if there is no favorite toy leave out all of them in favor of stories or imaginary games.

28. CARRY KID FRIENDLY SNACKS

Create a small snack counter in your bag to store away quick bites for those sudden hunger pangs. Depending on the child's age this could include chocolates, raisins, dry fruits, granola bars or biscuits. Also keep a bottle of water handy for your little one.

These things do not add much weight and can be adjusted in a handbag or knapsack.

29. GAMES TO CARRY

Create some travel specific, imaginary games if you have slightly grown up children, like spot the attractions. Keep a coloring book and colors handy for in-flight or hotel time. Apps on your smart phone can keep the children engaged with cartoons and story books. Older children are often entertained by games available on phones or tablets. This cuts the weight of luggage down while keeping the kids entertained.

30. LET THE KIDS CARRY THEIR LOAD

A good thing is to start early sharing of responsibilities. Let your child pick a bag of his or her choice and pack it themselves. Keep tabs on what they are stuffing in their bags by asking if they will be using that item on the trip. It could start out being just an entertainment bag initially but with growing years they will learn to sort the useful from the superfluous. Children as little as four can maneuver a small trolley suitcase like a pro- their experience in pull along toys credit. If you are worried that you may be pulling it for them, you may want to start with a backpack.

31. DECIDE ON LOCATION FOR CHILDREN TO SLEEP

While on a trip you might not always get a crib at your destination, and carrying one will make life all the more difficult. Instead call ahead to see if there are any cribs or roll out beds for children. You may even put blankets on the floor. Weave them a story about camping and they will gladly sleep without any trouble.

32. GET BABY PRODUCTS DELIVERED AT YOUR DESTINATION

If you are absolutely paranoid about not getting your favourite variety of diaper or brand of baby food, check out online stores like amazon.com for services in your destination city. You can buy things online ahead of your travel and get them delivered to your hotel upon arrival.

33. FEEDING NEEDS OF YOUR INFANTS

If you are travelling with a breastfed infant, you save the trouble of carrying bottles and bottle sanitization kits. For special food, or medications, you may need to call ahead to make sure you have a refrigerator where you are staying.

34. FEEDING NEEDS OF YOUR TODDLER

With the progression from infancy to toddler, their dietary requirements too evolve. You will have to pack some snacks for travelling time. Fresh fruits and vegetables can be purchased at your destination. Most of the cities you travel to in whichever part of the world, will have baby food products and formulas, available at the local drug-store or the supermarket.

35. PICKING CLOTHES FOR YOUR BABY

Contrary to popular belief, babies can do without many changes of clothes. At the most pack 2 outfits per day. Pack mix and match type clothes for your little one as well. Pick things which are comfortable to wear and quick to dry.

36. SELECTING SHOES FOR YOUR BABY

Like outfits, kids can make do with two pairs of comfortable shoes. If you can get some water resistant shoes it will be best. To expedite drying wet shoes, you can stuff newspaper in them then wrap them with newspaper and leave them to dry overnight.

37. KEEP ONE CHANGE OF CLOTHES HANDY

Travelling with kids can be tricky. Keep a change of clothes for the kids and mum handy in your purse or tote bag. This takes a bit of space in your hand luggage but comes extremely handy in case there are any accidents or spills.

38. LEAVE BEHIND BABY ACCESSORIES

Baby accessories like their bed, bath tub, car seat, crib etc. should be left at home. Many hotels provide a crib on request, while car seats can be borrowed from friends or rented. Babies can be given a bath in the hotel sink or even in the adult bath tub with a little bit of water. If you bring a few bath toys, they can be used in the bath, pool, and out of water. They can also be sanitized easily in the sink.

39. CARRY A SMALL LOAD OF PLASTIC BAGS

With children around there are chances of a number of soiled clothes and diapers. These plastic bags help to sort the dirt from the clean inside your big bag.

These are very light weight and come in handy to other carry stuff as well at times.

PACK WITH A PURPOSE

40. PACKING FOR BUSINESS TRIPS

One neutral-colored suit should suffice. It can be paired with different shirts, ties and accessories for different occasions. One pair of black suit pants could be worn with a matching jacket for the office or with a snazzy top for dinner.

41. PACKING FOR A CRUISE

Most cruises have formal dinners, and that formal dress usually takes up a lot of space. However you might find a tuxedo to rent. For women, a short black dress with multiple accessory options will do the trick.

42. PACKING FOR A LONG TRIP OVER DIFFERENT CLIMATES

The secret packing mantra for travel over multiple climates is layering. Layering traps air around your body creating insulation against the cold. The same

145

light t-shirt that is comfortable in a warmer climate can be the innermost layer in a colder climate.

REDUCE SOME MORE WEIGHT

43. LEAVE PRECIOUS THINGS AT HOME

Things that you would hate to lose or get damaged leave them at home. Precious jewelry, expensive gadgets or dresses, could be anything. You will not require these on your trip. Leave them at home and spare the load on your mind.

44. SEND SOUVENIRS BY MAIL

If you have spent all your money on purchasing souvenirs, carrying them back in the same bag that you brought along would be difficult. Either pack everything in another bag and check it in the airport or get everything shipped to your home. Use an international carrier for a secure transit, but this could be more expensive than the checking fees at the airport.

45. AVOID CARRYING BOOKS

Books equal to weight. There are many reading apps which you can download on your smart phone or tab.

Plus there are gadgets like Kindle and Nook that are thinner and lighter alternatives to your regular book.

CHECK, GET, SET, CHECK AGAIN

46. STRATEGIZE BEFORE PACKING

Create a travel list and prepare all that you think you need to carry along. Keep everything on your bed or floor before packing and then think through once again – do I really need that? Any item that meets this question can be avoided. Remove whatever you don't really need and pack the rest.

47. TEST YOUR LUGGAGE

Once you have fully packed for the trip take a test trip with your luggage. Take your bags and go to town for window shopping for an hour. If you enjoy your hour long trip it is good to go, if not, go home and reduce the load some more. Repeat this test till you hit the right weight.

48. ADD A ROLL OF DUCT TAPE

You might wonder why, when this book has been talking about reducing stuff, we're suddenly asking you to pack something totally unusual. This is because when you have limited supplies, duct tape is immensely helpful for small repairs – a broken bag, leaking zip-lock bag, broken sunglasses, you name it and duct tape can fix it, temporarily.

49. LIST OF ESSENTIAL ITEMS

Even though the emphasis is on packing light, there are things which have to be carried for any trip. Here is our list of essentials:

•Passport/Visa or any other ID

•Any other paper work that might be required on a trip like permits, hotel reservation confirmations etc.

•Medicines – all your prescription medicines and emergency kit, especially if you are travelling with children

•Medical or vaccination records

•Money in foreign currency if travelling to a different country

•Tickets- Email or Message them to your phone

50. MAKE THE MOST OF YOUR TRIP

Wherever you are going, whatever you hope to do we encourage you to embrace it whole-heartedly. Take in the scenery, the culture and above all, enjoy your time away from home.

On a long journey even a straw weighs heavy.

-Spanish Proverb

PACKING AND PLANNING TIPS

A Week before Leaving

- Arrange for someone to take care of pets and water plants.

- Stop mail and newspaper.

- Notify Credit Card companies where you are going.

- Change your thermostat settings.

- Car inspected, oil is changed, and tires have the correct pressure.

- Passports and photo identification is up to date.

- Pay bills.

- Copy important items and download travel Apps.

- Start collecting small bills for tips.

Right Before Leaving

- Clean out refrigerator.

- Empty garbage cans.

- Lock windows.

- Make sure you have the proper identification with you.

- Bring cash for tips.

- Remember travel documents.

- Lock door behind you.

- Remember wallet.

- Unplug items in house and pack chargers.

151

READ OTHER
GREATER THAN A TOURIST
BOOKS

Greater Than a Tourist San Miguel de Allende Guanajuato Mexico: 50 Travel Tips from a Local by Tom Peterson

Greater Than a Tourist – Lake George Area New York USA: 50 Travel Tips from a Local by Janine Hirschklau

Greater Than a Tourist – Monterey California United States: 50 Travel Tips from a Local by Katie Begley

Greater Than a Tourist – Chanai Crete Greece: 50 Travel Tips from a Local by Dimitra Papagrigoraki

Greater Than a Tourist – The Garden Route Western Cape Province South Africa: 50 Travel Tips from a Local by Li-Anne McGregor van Aardt

Greater Than a Tourist – Sevilla Andalusia Spain: 50 Travel Tips from a Local by Gabi Gazon

Greater Than a Tourist – Kota Bharu Kelantan Malaysia: 50 Travel Tips from a Local by Aditi Shukla

Children's Book: Charlie the Cavalier Travels the World by Lisa Rusczyk

153

> TOURIST

Visit Greater Than a Tourist for Free Travel Tips
http://GreaterThanATourist.com

Sign up for the Greater Than a Tourist Newsletter for
discount days, new books, and travel information:
http://eepurl.com/cxspyf

Follow us on Facebook for tips, images, and ideas:
https://www.facebook.com/GreaterThanATourist

Follow us on Pinterest for travel tips and ideas:
http://pinterest.com/GreaterThanATourist

Follow us on Instagram for beautiful travel images:
http://Instagram.com/GreaterThanATourist

>TOURIST

> TOURIST

At Greater Than a Tourist, we love to share travel tips with you. How did we do? What guidance do you have for how we can give you better advice for your next trip? Please send your feedback to GreaterThanaTourist@gmail.com as we continue to improve the series. We appreciate your constructive feedback. Thank you.

METRIC CONVERSIONS

TEMPERATURE

110° F —
100° F —   — 40° C
90° F —
80° F —   — 30° C
70° F —   — 20° C
60° F —
50° F —   — 10° C
40° F —
32° F —   — 0° C
20° F —
10° F —   — -10° C
0° F —
-10° F —   — -18° C
-20° F —   — -30° C

To convert F to C:

Subtract 32, and then multiply by 5/9 or .5555.

To Convert C to F:

Multiply by 1.8 and then add 32.

32F = 0C

LIQUID VOLUME

To Convert:.................Multiply by
U.S. Gallons to Liters............... 3.8
U.S. Liters to Gallons 26
Imperial Gallons to U.S. Gallons 1.2
Imperial Gallons to Liters....... 4.55
Liters to Imperial Gallons 22
1 Liter = .26 U.S. Gallon
1 U.S. Gallon = 3.8 Liters

DISTANCE

To convert ....Multiply by
Inches to Centimeters 2.54
Centimeters to Inches 39
Feet to Meters...................... .3
Meters to Feet 3.28
Yards to Meters 91
Meters to Yards 1.09
Miles to Kilometers 1.61
Kilometers to Miles............ .62
1 Mile = 1.6 km
1 km = .62 Miles

WEIGHT

1 Ounce = .28 Grams
1 Pound = .4555 Kilograms
1 Gram = .04 Ounce
1 Kilogram = 2.2 Pounds

TRAVEL QUESTIONS

- Do you bring presents home to family or friends after a vacation?

- Do you get motion sick?

- Do you have a favorite billboard?

- Do you know what to do if there is a flat tire?

- Do you like a sun roof open?

- Do you like to eat in the car?

- Do you like to wear sun glasses in the car?

- Do you like toppings on your ice cream?

- Do you use public bathrooms?

- Did you bring your cell phone and does it have power?

- Do you have a form of identification with you?

- Have you ever been pulled over by a cop?

- Have you ever given money to a stranger on a road trip?

- Have you ever taken a road trip with animals?

- Have you ever went on a vacation alone?

- Have you ever run out of gas?

- If you could move to any place in the world, where would it be?

- If you could travel anywhere in the world, where would you travel?

- If you could travel in any vehicle, which one would it be?

- If you had three things to wish for from a magic genie, what would they be?

- If you have a driver's license, how many times did it take you to pass the test?

- What are you the most afraid of on vacation?

- What do you want to get away from the most when you are on vacation?

- What foods smells bad to you?

- What item do you bring on ever trip with you away from home?

- What makes you sleepy?

- What song would you love to hear on the radio when you're cruising on the highway?

- What travel job would you want the least?

- What will you miss most while you are away from home?

- What is something you always wanted to try?

- What is the best road side attraction that you ever saw?

- What is the farthest distance you ever biked?

- What is the farthest distance you ever walked?

- What is the weirdest thing you needed to buy while on vacation?

- What is your favorite candy?

- What is your favorite color car?

- What is your favorite family vacation?

- What is your favorite food?

- What is your favorite gas station drink or food?

- What is your favorite license plate design?

- What is your favorite restaurant?

- What is your favorite smell?

- What is your favorite song?

- What is your favorite sound that nature makes?

- What is your favorite thing to bring home from a vacation?

- What is your favorite vacation with friends?

- What is your favorite way to relax?

- Where is the farthest place you ever traveled in a car?

- Where is the farthest place you ever went North, South, East and West?

- Where is your favorite place in the world?

- Who is your favorite singer?

- Who taught you how to drive?

- Who will you miss the most while you are away?

- Who if the first person you will contact when you get to your destination?

- Who brought you on your first vacation?

- Who likes to travel the most in your life?

- Would you rather be hot or cold?

- Would you rather drive above, below, or at the speed limited?

- Would you rather drive on a highway or a back road?

- Would you rather go on a train or a boat?

- Would you rather go to the beach or the woods?

TRAVEL BUCKET LIST

1.

2.

3.

4.

5.

6.

7.

8.

9.

10.

NOTES

51955402R00110

Made in the USA
San Bernardino, CA
04 September 2019